WHAT'S
RIGHT
With
ME?

WHAT'S RIGHT

With

ME?

Hope for the Dyslexic

JOAN STAMBAUGH

ACKNOWLEDGEMENTS

This book would not have been possible without those who were willing to share their stories and their lives, giving better understanding to the way they think and process print. Their talent and resourcefulness have inspired me as I see them forge through life with a persistence and stamina that far surpass most; all while fighting false assumptions that paint them as *slow* or *lazy* or *dumb*. Thank you to those who were willing to be interviewed, and to those who shared their stories through other sources. It is you who bring encouragement to others in desperate need of understanding.

I am also grateful for the many parents of dyslexic children who have jumped on the advocacy band wagon, going to great lengths and personal sacrifice to help their children. Some of you I had the privilege of talking to personally, and others were willing to share their experiences through the Fundamental Learning Center and Decoding Dyslexia— NJ. You bring validity and heart to the realities of dyslexia.

My sincere thanks to others who are writing, interviewing, listening to, and advocating for those with dyslexia.

It is your work that kept me motivated and sure that this message needs to get out. To name a few: Sally Shaywitz, who brought scientific evidence to the forefront; Brock and Fernette Eide, who make it abundantly clear that dyslexia is not necessarily a bad thing in light of strong hidden potentials; Harvey Hubbell, who brings enlightenment and encouragement through his countless interviews; and Philip Schultz and Steven Milner, who take us into the heart of dyslexia with personal experiences. Without your work, this project would not have been possible.

I owe my greatest debt of gratitude to the wonderful staff and volunteers at the Fundamental Learning Center. Thank you for the countless hours you spend to educate teachers, parents, children, and the community. You have changed many lives, including mine, as you took me from a state of disillusionment to one of hope.

A special thanks also to Laura Robinson whose encouragement and guidance in the beginning of the writing process took me from muddling through to feeling empowered. You helped me see that this message could change lives.

But perhaps the biggest encouragement has come from my family—my husband, my children, and my parents.

Thank you for your belief in me. And thanks to my Mom for telling me "*You* can do that!" when I first shared the prospect of writing, and for inspiring me with the talent you demonstrated in your autobiography as a sophomore in high school.

And finally, I would be remiss if I didn't acknowledge how God prodded me forward, giving me a sense of hope, direction, and passion throughout the process. There would have been many times when I would have given up if it weren't for God's gentle, but consistent compassion toward the misunderstood. He is why I care about children who are struggling in our classrooms and the impact it has on their lives.

CONTENTS

—◄•►—

Unless someone like you cares a whole awful lot, nothing is going to get better. It's not.

—Dr. Seuss' *The Lorax*

INTRODUCTION

Throughout many of our schools today, you will hear teachers whisper the D-word in hushed tones. They are speaking of dyslexia—the name of a specific learning disability that is frowned upon from being used in discussions or in writing. It is a learning difference so full of misunderstanding and confusion that many professionals think they're better off ignoring it rather than making yet another change to a system already under scrutiny.

Given the fact that 20 percent of our population is affected to some degree with dyslexia, the shroud of mystery is surprising in our society's love of diagnosis. Part of the mystery of dyslexia is that even though it can be diagnosed and treated and explained by scientific research, many who are dyslexic don't know why they can't do what their classmates can easily do, and they are left behind to struggle. Ultimately, dyslexia is a person and is best described by each person who deals with it on a daily basis. Each person who grapples with its challenges also has strengths that can help them rise above the stigma of having a learning disability.

The success stories of famous characters from history, such as Thomas Edison and Albert Einstein, are oft-told and well-known. Lesser known is the fact that both of them had dyslexia. "A teacher sent the following note home with a six-year-old boy: 'He is too stupid to learn.' That boy was Thomas A. Edison." Likewise, it was said of Albert Einstein that he had "difficulty learning to read, poor rote memory for math facts, and lifelong difficulty with spelling."

Lesser known, too, are the stories of the students and parents that I share with you. I have a passion that drives me in this journey: It is that the silent stigma attached to their heartache will disappear in light of the hope and encouragement shared by others who have dyslexia, those who have the giftedness and fortitude to fight through when the going gets tough.

In this book, I invite you to journey with me as we seek to understand the misunderstood. Our journey will center around the stories of those with dyslexia, both those who are still struggling through the day-to-day traditional class-room setting, and those who have successfully maneuvered through. Their stories will give us insight as we learn from them; how they found hope and healing through the help of proper diagnosis and tailored treatment. The names of some have been changed for their protection.

Their inspirational stories may bring us hope, but we also need the tools necessary for change. We can't continue to ignore the emotional impact on students and their families when they are put into a one-size-fits-all slot. We need to recognize that each of us has a unique set of learning needs and strengths. Studies dating back to the 1930s give us the evidence needed to move forward with identification, the best practices for remediation, and a better understanding of differing brain processing, including common strengths that long to be expressed. Helping the dyslexic student discover their strengths, which often gives them an "outside the box" kind of thinking, instead of a "conform to the norm" kind of thinking, could give us the next great thinker, like Albert Einstein or Thomas Edison.

The first step is gaining knowledge, an easy step that can have a profound effect in the life of a child who is struggling in school. In each chapter, we will debunk a myth surrounding dyslexia, which is conveyed in the first line of each chapter title, and replace it with facts that can further enlighten. But more important than the facts are the lives that are deeply affected. So please come with me as we walk a mile in the shoes of Jeanine, Cooper, Justin, Anna, Dalton, Nicole, Kristi, Shaun, Drayton, and Sally. They speak for millions of others.

TEN COMMON MYTHS
SURROUNDING DYSLEXIA

1

—◄•►—

? Reading Ability = Intelligence ?
Our Distorted View of Intelligence

My Story: Defining Ourselves

I can still picture the distorted contortions of my brother's face when he removed his teeth to reveal the "bitter beer face," a look similar to the toothless hillbilly. Our family would erupt with laughter as we identified his look with the then-popular Keystone Beer commercials. The nineties advertisement definitely got the TV watcher's attention, just as my brother often grabbed the limelight at family gatherings. A question asked of me many times after we both grew up and moved away from our hometown speaks to his winning personality. "What's your brother up to these days? I sure miss him."

I often envied my brother Tom's outgoing, fun-loving spirit, which drew many to him. I, on the other hand, was more on the shy side and had to force myself to approach people and initiate conversation. Tom's magnetic, adventurous personality made him the life of the party, someone who could talk others into fun and sometimes mischievous acts.

I cannot tell you my story without telling you my brother's story, because while we were quite different, we had something in common. Both of us struggled with some aspects of our educations, and it is still unclear to me whether either of us have some degree of dyslexia. The complexity of dyslexia, especially with the varying multitude of symptoms and levels of severity, is a big reason why it continues to go unacknowledged in many of our schools today. I share our stories because we represent the vast number of children who are deeply affected by how they perceive themselves when school doesn't come easy. Not just those with dyslexia, but those who don't fit the *norm* or the child whose learning style doesn't match the teaching style. My brother and I also represent the wide range of how one copes with feelings of inferiority; I am alive today, he is not.

Despite having an average intelligence, Tom struggled to learn to read and write. He masked how much this bothered him by immersing himself into a strong social life and emotionally withdrawing from anything having to do with school. He became a pro at hiding the fact that he couldn't read or write well. During his teen years, he dealt with some depression, which combined with increasing insecurities, took him down a slippery slope. This fun-loving, people-magnet's identity was gradually ripped away by increasing self-doubt; I know because in his more serious moments, he told me he thought he was *stupid*. Any trace of positive self-image was further stolen by alcohol, which eventually took his life at the age of forty-six.

I also suffered for many years with a poor self-esteem due to reading issues. I often thought I didn't measure up because I was a slow reader and had to work extra hard, or at least longer than others, when studying. I assumed that slow reading was equated with low intelligence, and this thinking followed me into college and beyond. I envied those who seemed to pass classes without any studying—or at least without the blood, sweat, and tears that I endured. For this reason, I majored in special education since I was sure my struggles could be used to help others. But that was not the only reason I went this direction.

One memory from my middle school years in the late 1960s played a part in my career choice. In those days, we still had recess in middle school, during which time a girl in my class who had the label of mentally retarded was bullied. I witnessed name-calling and teasing almost daily and made the cowardly choice of turning a blind eye.

I was extremely self-conscious and shy and wouldn't think of standing up to the bullies at that point in my life. Yet I felt, and continue to feel, that I participated in the bully mentality because I didn't stick up for her.

Now I am in a place where I can fight for the underdog, stick up for the bullied, and, in my mind, make amends for my cowardly stance in middle school. But I discovered something even more detrimental to students, not just those in special education, but all students. The classroom has become so regimented by standardization that we've lost sight of each student's uniqueness—how they learn and process information—and the need to express their strengths. We spend most of our time fixing the weaknesses while ignoring or downplaying the strengths. Children are much more likely to buy into working on the difficult tasks if they can utilize their strengths to get there.

After several years of frustrations felt by students and myself, I decided to make a change. Teaching and learning the same old way and with a curriculum that didn't allow for diversification was not getting us anywhere. This crossroads brought two possibilities: getting my master's degree in a more generalized education program, or getting intense, specialized training that would apply in the classroom for those who struggle to learn through traditional methods. I took the less-traveled road: I enrolled in classes at the neighboring city's dyslexia center, the Fundamental

Learning Center of Wichita, Kansas. The next three years of classes were a game changer for me. I returned to the classroom more empowered and excited to use the multi-sensory teaching approaches I had learned. The students' responses and motivation gave me confirmation that I had made the right decision.

While my motivation for going to the Fundamental Learning Center was to help children learn, I found it helped me learn. Concepts and strategies I was learning helped me gain a renewed love of the written word, and a phonics program that made sense to me made teaching come alive. I don't remember ever being taught using formal phonics instruction and found it extremely beneficial. Also, I discovered that I am like many of my students; I am a visual/kinesthetic (hands-on) learner, and when taught through auditory methods only, I hear "wha wha wha wha" as depicted in Charlie Brown's cartoons when adults are talking. There was a time when teachers were told to teach according to a student's learning style. But that was a fad that has been pushed out to accommodate the stringent testing and curriculum demands.

I don't think the shy, reserved version of myself, when in middle school, would believe that she could ever advocate for others. But that is exactly what I hope to do by sharing these stories. People with dyslexia are often misunderstood and under-acknowledged, and they are being discriminated against when we continue to ignore the research. It is crucial that this changes for the sake of our children and our current illiteracy epidemic. It is crucial that this changes so that we stop the greatest epidemic of all—the loss of the gifts that all children, no matter their limitations or capabilities, come into the world to share.

> By failing to recognize the value of the slower but incredibly rich insight system, and instead placing all our emphasis on linear, rule-based, deductive thinking styles, we hinder the development of all children, but perhaps especially those who are the most creative and insight dependent. (Eide, 2011)

What is Intelligence?

"How did you get your answer, Cody?" his teacher asked him after solving a multistep math problem. The simple question is met by a head hung as low as his sagging pants. You see, he can't answer that question even though he did get the correct answer, and consequently, he is not given credit. Cody, a fifth grade student, already feels like a failure because he can barely read and write. And now, he feels like a failure in his favorite subject of math.

Cody is just one of many students I've worked with who would amaze me with higher level thinking skills, especially when it involved numbers. Cody just knew the answers to math application problems even though he struggled to work them out on paper, a problem in today's classroom. As we sat together working on math homework, I would discreetly work out the answer on paper in order to guide him through the process. After multiple steps and finally reaching the correct answer, I would look up at him only to find his page blank. Without seeing how I solved the problem, he would blurt out the answer, and more often than not, his answer matched mine. Where he fell short, according to some, was not being able to show any work or prove how he figured it out. Many teachers require students to show their work because that is now an expectation on state assessments. Consequently, a strength can become a weakness in a child's mind unless there is some flexibility with expectations and encouragement in the process.

Every day in the classroom, I saw what it did to those children who learn differently than their peers. We inadvertently categorize the students who aren't learning at the same pace or who can't demonstrate mastery like their classmates seem to do so easily. Our view of intelligence when it comes to reading and writing is often limited to the ability to fluently read, complete paper/pencil tasks, and take tests. For those who struggle, we put them in the *slow* group, whether by grouping them together in the classroom or placing them in special education services or in some type of intervention group. We say, without words, that they aren't as smart as others. Actually, they see themselves as different from their peers and begin labeling themselves.

When we're young, we often see many aspects of our world from a black-white perspective. We look at the social rules as right versus wrong, good versus bad. In the social hierarchy of our schools, children look at their classmates as either friend or not friend, smart or dumb. As we mature, this myth fades as we recognize how complex life can be.

Before coming to grips with the complexity of this world, we tend to resort to judging. We've all probably experienced and dished out some form of it at some time in our lives. Being over or under weight, an accentuated feature, a lack of athletic ability, or any number of ways we see ourselves or others as different can be fuel for ridicule. We lose sight of the face behind the difference. Unless we've walked in their shoes, we don't have a clue what they are going through or who they really are. Obviously, being critical toward others isn't limited to children. If we're honest with ourselves, many of us continue this mentality as adults. As we get older, perhaps it's the homeless person begging on the street corner, or the alcoholic going through rehab for the third time. In the classroom, it may be the child who is labeled lazy because they appear to stop trying, or the child who is considered bad because they can't just sit and listen to the teacher like others do.

In reality, learning and the potential of the brain is a very gray area, and we still have a great deal to learn about its mysteries. In education, we try to teach in a black-and-white style of thinking. Teachers and administrators have been told what and how students should be taught. We impart knowledge and hope students will memorize the facts or skills taught. Education has become over standardized to the detriment to our students. The new standard of teaching and measurement of skill mastery, the Common Core, is under a great deal of scrutiny today, partly because it requires students to show how problems are solved in order to receive full credit. The presumption that every child has the same learning style and should be able to demonstrate mastery in the same way leaves many behind. Cody is just one of many who can't explain or show how he comes up with correct answers, and this is particularly true for most who have dyslexia. The educational system has been reduced to a factory style of regurgitation of information with everyone using the same process to get from point A to point B.

"No, your son can't do things in a slightly different way, all the kids have to learn it the same way." This remark came from a teacher as she addressed the parent of a student who was struggling in her classroom. With further questioning, she responds to the "why?" with, "Because that's how we've always done it."

Teachers have been stripped of the freedom to teach to students' unique strengths and weaknesses. Testing demands have caused most to teach content required of them in order to pass the test instead of teaching in a way that students catch the spirit of becoming a lifelong learner.

In the classroom, we often try to oversimplify how we learn and even the stages of development. We try to force children onto the treadmill according to their age, and they have to either keep up or get left behind. Life would be so much simpler if we lived in a black-and-white world. If that were the case, each person would learn at the same rate, have the same learning style, and be ready to progress to increasingly more difficult concepts at the same pace.

So what is intelligence? A simple definition of intelligence is "the ability to acquire and apply knowledge and skills." This fits with how we usually view it in the classroom. However, this definition doesn't explain those children who struggle with basic skills while possessing strengths that often exceed others, even those who are considered better students. Intelligence can be better understood as the representation of the brain's functioning power, which manifests differing strengths and weaknesses to varying degrees. Complex? Yes, but perhaps more accurate. Can we say that someone with left brain dominance is smarter than someone with right brain dominance? Left brain dominance gives us the ability to perform tasks with greater precision, accuracy, speed, and automaticity. Right brain dominance is the creative, inventive side that helps us get the big picture and gives us inferential reasoning. But just because we may demonstrate dominance on one side doesn't mean the other is absent. Intelligence is much more than regurgitating facts and performing skills.

The traditional intelligence quotient (IQ) testing can give us a view of overall intelligence, and it can give a fairly accurate reading, but it is far from a comprehensive diagnostic tool. It is not designed to measure the varying capabilities. Perhaps forms of measurement can be updated now that we have a constant influx of new technology. Tom West, the author of a Pulitzer Prize–winning nonfiction book entitled *The Soul of a New Machine* gives insight into the possibility of using technology for measurement of the brain's capabilities.

> Some business people can anticipate things. Some athletes always seem to be where the ball is going to be because they can model in their minds what's going to happen and speed it up. This is an extension of that visual-spatial capacity, but how on earth do we measure these things? I think that with new technologies, we can work out ways of measuring, but it will require new tools. The old pencil and paper and rotations in your mind will be inad-

equate..... Our culture has been tied to an old technology of text and books, but this new technology is going to change the rules of the game. (Tom West, as quoted in Hubbell, 2012)

Our educational system needs to keep up with the times as our society continues to make advances in technology and in the science of the brain. Our limited perspective of intelligence is partially due to an emphasis on measurement rather than on how we actually learn. Our black-and-white perspective of intelligence needs a major overhaul for the sake of all children, but especially for the child who thinks and learns differently.

––––––––––––

Myth: People with dyslexia lack intelligence.
Busted:

Dyslexia is not an intellectual disability, since dyslexia and IQ are not interrelated, as a result of cognition developing independently. (Ferrer, E, Shaywitz, BA, Holahan, JM, Marchione, K, Shaywitz, SE. January 2010 Psychol. Sci.)

Dyslexia creates reading problems, not impairment of thinking, failure of imagination or deficiency of courage. (Dr. Linda G. Tessler)

2

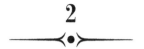

? Seeing Backwards = Dyslexia ?

A Look at Dyslexia

Jeanine's Story: A Look Back
Leads to a Push Forward

I wish I could be in the 'Hummingbird Group,' Jeanine thought as she looked jealously at Susie, the smart girl whose desk sat next to hers. Jeanine was in the crow group, the reading group for dummies, in her mind. These were not the actual names for the reading groups, but Jeanine's memories hold the strong emotions of differences being accentuated and not in a positive way.

It was the 1960s, the era of the "Dick and Jane" curriculum. Memorization of sight words was how reading was taught. Jeanine remembers the daily flash cards, fearing the time when the picture cues would be removed from the sight-word cards. When that day came, she wondered how anybody could figure out the display of markings called letters, which to her was gibberish.

There was one thing Jeanine felt she could do well; she was a super fast runner, an ability that earned her the respect of the boys. She was the happiest when in gym class and on the playground. At least her natural athletic ability was something she could be proud of. This was not the case in the classroom. All she wanted was to please the teacher, which seemed impossible.

When Jeanine was in the second grade, she remembers imitating Susie, the pretty girl who sat next to her, to make it look like she was reading. She would watch Susie move her finger along the gibberish, and Jeanine began mimicking this movement along with turning the pages in sync with her desk partner. They were eventually assigned as reading partners, and Jeanine would listen as her partner read aloud. While this didn't do anything to help her learn to read, it did help get her through the day. Jeanine found herself daydreaming. *If we could cut off the tops of our heads, I bet our brains would look different.* This was a profound thought at the time, and she now knows it's true. Their brains did look very different.

Jeanine was the firstborn of four, born into a family rich in academia with higher education as the strong expectation. Her father graduated with a doctorate from Harvard University followed by a career as Dean of Business at Wichita State University. Her mother graduated with a degree in English. School was easy for her parents, so when Jeanine was having difficulty learning to read, spell, and memorize math facts, they didn't understand. The frustrations were great for both Jeanine and her parents, and the dissent became particularly accentuated when her dad hired an after-school tutor in the third grade. Watching her friends play kickball outside the window while being stuck inside learning phonics with "Miss Stinky Breath" temporarily knocked her dad off the pedestal she had placed him on. On the first day of tutoring, Jeanine felt further confirmation of shame when her tutor pulled out an acrylic box of letter tiles, blew the dust off, and said, "Boy, I haven't had to use these in a long time." Even though going to a tutor wasn't how Jeanine wanted to spend her time, she eventually realized she was slowly learning to read with the use of phonics instruction. The skills necessary for writing, however, did not come until much later.

The phonics instruction helped, but reading continued to be slow and laborious with pressure to complete work in a timely manner making school increasingly more difficult. Getting good grades was important to Jeanine's parents; bad grades led to being grounded. Not a happy dilemma for this middle school socialite who only found happiness in sports and her relationships with friends. After spending most of her seventh grade year grounded, Jeanine resolved to change her predicament. She decided to work harder, even into the wee hours of the night. She began secretly bringing her studies to bed with her, way past her bed time, creating a mini-fort with her blankets and studying by flashlight. The click of her flashlight would provide a quick exit if anyone would decide to enter. Working hard helped some, but to assure grades that would allow her to spend time with friends, Jeanine matter-of-factly states, "In eighth grade, I also perfected cheating."

While cheating became a temporary fix to issues that affected her social life, Jeanine eventually saw its futility. She began perfecting another skill that would ultimately change her life and the lives of thousands. Although Jeanine continued to struggle with academics, she was learning to stand up for herself and push herself when life gets tough. Her determination and perseverance were evident in a conversation with her guidance counselor after taking an aptitude test in the ninth grade. Jeanine started the conversation by telling him, "It's not a matter of what I want to be when I grow up, I will be a veterinarian." When he came back with, "That's not what my paper says," Jeanine appallingly responded with, "Well, what does your stupid paper say?" With a smirk on his face, he replied, "Your test shows that you should be a car mechanic because you're not smart enough to go to college." Until this time, Jeanine never had even a seed of doubt about achieving what she wanted. So she took the counselor's harsh words and kicked her determination up a notch.

With college in her future, Jeanine took the SAT and got one of the worst scores in her high school. She was too embarrassed to tell anyone that she was only able to finish about half of the timed tests, so she nonchalantly acted like she just blew it off when questioned by her dad. Of course, this led to taking it a second time. Jeanine had to come up with a strategy for the second go-around, so she decided cheating was the only way she could actually complete the test. The first step was to look for the smart-looking guy with pencil-filled pockets. After seating herself next to him, she proceeded to discreetly fill in the same circles on the machine-readable response sheet, only to find at the end of the first test she was off by one. So much for that strategy! Jeanine took the rest of the tests on her own at her own pace, but when the time was almost up, she filled in the bubbles hoping for good odds. She did have a better score the second time, but felt that if she had been given all the time she needed, it would have been a more accurate measurement of her actual intelligence.

In college, Jeanine continued to struggle, failing her first field of study in the school of occupational therapy at the University of Kansas. Her parents stepped in to move her back home where she attended Wichita State University. Learning from her first experience, she changed majors from occupational therapy to education and planned out how to go forward. She found her pace by taking three classes per semester, two tough ones and one fluff class, and ended her college career with a 4.0 grade point average.

It was not until her senior year in college that Jeanine would have answers to the years of struggle. One day her reading practicum teacher shared that he suspected she had dyslexia after looking at the quality of her writing. With this simple word, *dyslexia*, and his affirmation of her strong work ethic, came an instant relief and the first-time thought of *maybe I'm not dumb after all!* Wanting to reach out and hug him, she restrained herself and instead questioned him further. "What does this mean, and how will it affect my future?" His response took her by surprise, but also gave some much needed encouragement. "I can't say for sure what it is since there is very little research on it other than people with dyslexia see letters and words backwards." Although she knew she didn't really see backwards, she recognized that her professor was onto something, and she vowed to learn more. He went on to say, "I know you must have worked extremely hard to get to this point." Finally someone acknowledged her hard work and gave her a glimmer of hope. She was excited to share this with her parents, but it was met with disbelief. In their eyes, dyslexia meant a lack of intelligence, and that didn't fit the daughter they now saw as bright despite the difficulties with learning like others. Jeanine asked them, "Well, what did you call it?" Her dad's response took her by surprise. "We just thought you were flakey!"

This was their first conversation about Jeanine's struggles in school, because they didn't want to say anything that would hurt her or affect her self-esteem. However, with knowledge comes freedom, and after finally having a name for the struggles, Jeanine could pursue more information. She learned that there actually was a large amount of research on dyslexia, and it doesn't have anything to do with seeing backwards. Gaining knowledge brought her a peace and self-acceptance that she never had before, and this eventually turned into a vision that is now impacting thousands. Her expertise and compassion for others with dyslexia grew into founding the Fundamental Learning Center, an educational not-for-profit center, serving children with significant reading, spelling, and writing difficulties, including children with dyslexia.

A common description of those with dyslexia is their ability to think outside the box, but Jeanine described one of her strengths as being able to "talk my way out of a box." She sees this as one of the keys to her survival of school. Add determination, perseverance, and savvy social skills, and there's no place to go but forward. This gift of communication includes an ability to read moods and body language, and therefore, empathize with other. These skills led to an ability to talk her way into hearts for the advocacy of those who are struggling to learn through traditional methods. Jeanine uses her personal experience with dyslexia, past and present, to bring hope and encouragement to those still stuck in the cycle of self-doubt. Compassion, coupled with outside-the-box thinking and talking, is resulting in amazing advances to bring research validated literacy instruction to children, as well as educating parents and the educational community.

A look at Jeanine's past gives us a glimpse into how she dealt with the difficult aspects of her own education, as well as the importance of embracing the strengths that strongly counterbalance the weaknesses. Having the facts about dyslexia has been instrumental in her push forward. In addition to becoming an expert in the field for the benefit of thousands of families and teachers, her experience and knowledge turned her son Cooper's life around as we'll see in chapter 3. But first, let's explore what dyslexia looks like.

What Does Dyslexia Look Like?

"I would see letters, but never recognize them as a word," he explains. "The little words could be the worst. Then if I got it, I didn't recognize the word when I saw it the next time. They were like pieces of a puzzle that I couldn't make into a picture." (The Yale Center for Dyslexia & Creativity; http:// dyslexia.yale.edu)

These are the words of Nelsan Ellis, an actor known for many roles, but most recently his portrayal of Martin Luther King Jr. in *The Butler*. In his acting career, it takes longer for him to study and memorize the material, but he says, "Once I've got it, I've got it. I always have a different perspective and my mind is like a vault. I memorize like a beast."

Success stories such as his are awe-inspiring, especially in light of Ellis regarding himself as retarded when it came to school. He recalls his second grade teacher who recognized that he had dyslexia, and therefore tutored him daily when his classmates went to PE. Unfortunately, this was the only support and understanding throughout the remainder of Ellis's education. His family was too poor to pay for private programs or tutoring, so the negative self-perception stayed with him throughout his schooling. What perseverance in the face of such a difficult beginning!

If you are reading this, then you probably know someone who has dyslexia, or you have someone in mind who you suspect to be dyslexic. Or perhaps it's you! Whoever you are, knowledge is the first step. So let's look at what dyslexia looks like according to the experts in the field and those who are in the trenches, whether it is the child with dyslexia or the one fighting to help their child, grandchild, or student. One mother's plea for help after watching her son's frustrations year after year was expressed as a poem. She speaks for so many who are experiencing similar struggles.

> *Sean's* problems with school started in pre-school.
> He doesn't know his colors.
> Work with him.
> Check his eyes, is he colorblind?
> No. His eyes are fine.
> He doesn't know his ABC's.
> Work with him.
> Send him to kindergarten.
> He may have to repeat kindergarten.
> Repeat kindergarten.
> Constant ear infections.
> Check his ears.
> Can't write his name.
> Writes his letters backwards.
> Watching him write is painful.
> Work with him.
> Can't read.
> Can't read sight words.
> Can't do spelling tests
> NO MORE SPELLING TESTS!!!

Please, no more spelling tests!
Work with him.
Tubes, tonsils, and adenoids out! Maybe that will help!
Title 1, qualifies, doesn't qualify, and qualifies again!
Not reading at level.
Barely reading at all. Pretends to read.
Work with him.
Homework, homework, homework.
Hidden in the desk.
Don't deal with it, just hide it!
NO MORE SPELLING TESTS!!!
Can't go to school, I'm sick.
My stomach hurts.
I have a headache.
How many more days of school?
Do I have school today?
Do I have to go to school today?
No school, no school, no school!
Test him....
For what? Where?

"Been there!" you say. Some say, "There now! HELP!!" Help begins with knowing if it really is dyslexia that is making school so difficult. If it is, there is good news. While dyslexia is never outgrown, there are strategies that can be taught to help manage it, which we will look at in chapter 3. But first, identification begins with knowing its definition and the signs of dyslexia.

There are many misconceptions surrounding dyslexia, with some of the more common myths pointed out in the chapter titles. There are also several definitions that can give us a snapshot of what dyslexia looks like, but one in particular captures a more complete picture of the person who is commonly referred to as learning disabled. That definition comes from Dr. Brian Stone.

Dr. Stone, a licensed psychologist with expertise in this field, dedicates his profession to the testing of individuals with suspected dyslexia and is one of the few in his area qualified to give a formal diagnosis. There is a great need for more qualified psychologists, demonstrated by Dr. Stone's lengthy waiting list. He says,

> Dyslexia: A weakness in a sea of strengths—an inherited neurological condition that makes word reading and / or reading fluency difficult (a brain-based pattern of strengths and weaknesses that makes reading more difficult than it should be for someone so bright). Difficulty with the most basic part of language: sounds—keeping them in order, applying them to letters consistently, quickly remembering and writing letters—yet excelling at much higher level thinking and understanding.

Before delving into the weaknesses, it is important to recognize the "sea of strengths" found in so many who have dyslexia. There are numerous examples of amazing success stories, those who would survive the failures of school. Novelist Vince Flynn gives us a glimpse into a surprising strength despite being considered a failure when it came to school.

> "I was a naturally gifted chess player. It was a weird, weird, weird deal: even though I was failing in school, I could always just see in advance how the game would unfold."
>
> —Eide (2011)

Flynn used this innate gift of prediction in many of his novels. Prior to 9/11, he saw Islamic radical fundamentalism as one of the biggest threats to national security. This motivated him to write three novels based around this premise, and all were published before the tragic events of 9/11. Flynn's ability to predict became evident as a child, when he played chess with some of the best players in the Twin Cities, a gift that proved to spur him on to become one of the most well-known novelists of our time.

Chapter 7 is devoted to common strengths shared by those with dyslexia. I share Vince's unique gift at this point in order to emphasize that weaknesses alone should not encompass how we define the individual with dyslexia. This needs to be at the forefront of our thinking as we tackle the common signs of dyslexia.

Equally important is recognizing that just as each of us is unique and complex, so too is the dyslexic. Some are highly intelligent, some are not. Some have learned how to compensate and their dyslexia barely affects them, some are so deeply affected that they believe they can't ever climb out of the "failure stigma." Some exhibit only a few of the following indicators, some struggle with almost all of them, and in varying degrees.

Signs of Dyslexia

Preschool

1. Delayed speech.

> After researching both ADD and dyslexia, we noticed Jenni has several red flag symptoms for dyslexia that we never knew were associated. A few examples are late talker, trouble learning to tie shoes, bed wetting, and difficulty learning address and phone number. (Parent)

2. Confusion of left versus right/late establishing a dominant hand.
3. Difficulty with learning to tie shoes.
4. Chronic ear infections.
5. Trouble memorizing address, phone number, or the alphabet.
6. Can't create words that rhyme.

> The first indication that there was something different was a simple car game where the family would take turns with rhyming—easy words, such as hat, cat, bat, but Kristi couldn't do it. (Kristi's Story)

7. A close relative who has dyslexia.

> Scientists say that if you are dyslexic, there is a 40 percent chance that you will have a dyslexic child. My daughter is dyslexic, happy, doing well, and proud to be on the team. When I looked into it, I found other family members who didn't always do well in school. But they did do very well in the outside world. (Harvey Hubbell, 2012)

Elementary School

1. Phonological awareness is the basic core deficit in dyslexia (see chapter 3 for more detailed description).

> Phonological awareness is an important and reliable predictor of later reading ability. Researchers report that 90% of the children with reading disabilities have trouble with accurate and fluent word recognition usually related to phonological awareness difficulties. (NICHD)

2. Slow, choppy, inaccurate reading.

> The problem started the first day in class when each child had to read out loud. When I started to read, the other children started to laugh because my reading was very slow....I would stutter when reading, and the other children's bullying brought on panic attacks.
> (Milner, 2012)

a. Guesses words based on shape or context

> Many times she will just guess what the next word in a
> sentence is instead of sounding it out. (Parent).

b. Skips or misreads small words, such as prepositions (*at, to, of*)

c. Ignores suffixes

d. Difficulty with sounding out unknown words

> He struggled to sound out the words…He looked at some
> of his sight words and read them backwards. (Parent)

e. Mixing up sounds or syllables in long words

> While doing research online I noticed Lizzy has some
> classic signs of dyslexia. For instance, when she looks
> at a word she often reads the middle or end instead of
> sounding out the first letter (ie. 'hopped' becomes 'open',
> 'saw' becomes 'was'). (Parent)

f. Can't remember sight words (*they*, *were*, *does*), homonyms (*their*, *there*, *they're*), or the same word from page to page.

> *Julie's* difficulties are puzzling because she is a very imaginative, sensitive child who uses a large vocabulary....I notice when reading at home that when she sounds a word out and reads it, she does not seem to remember the word when it then shows up on the very next page and she will then sound it out all over again.
>
> (Parent)

g. Comprehension is better when text is read to them

> It's important to recognize that not all problems with reading comprehension are caused by dyslexia. Students who read fluently and decode well but still comprehend poorly generally have other issues with attention or language. In contrast, students with dyslexia will generally show problems with decoding and fluency but will understand texts much better when hearing them read than when reading them themselves. (Eide, 2011)

3. Slow, non-automatic handwriting that is difficult to read (dysgraphia)

> Even individuals with dyslexia who ultimately become highly skilled writers will nearly always struggle early in school with the fine-detail features of writing. Though Blake Charlton is now an accomplished novelist, he struggled greatly with handwriting: "In special ed class I failed a lot of papers because the teacher couldn't read anything I wrote." (Eide, 2011)

a. Difficulty transitioning from print to cursive
b. Letter or number reversals continuing past the end of first grade

> When they first learn to write, many children will reverse not only symbols that have true mirrors (like p/q or b/d), but essentially all letters or numbers. For most children these mistakes begin to diminish after only a few repetitions. However, for some truly dyslexic children–in our experience roughly one in four – letter reversals can be a much more persistent and important problem.
> (Eide, 2011)

4. Poor written expression with large discrepancy between verbal skills and writing

> I knew that I was intelligent because I could do the work and see the answers in my mind but I could not put them on paper as other children could in the class.
> (Milner, 2012)

a. Terrible spelling

> When she practiced spelling, she would put letters in words that did not contain that particular sound. (Parent)

> They stopped looking at my spelling and started looking at the content of what I was writing. There was a revolution in my brain because they helped me see that I had good ideas—I just couldn't spell them right. (Eide, 2011)

b. Difficulty with punctuation when writing and ignoring punctuation when reading

5. When speaking, difficulty finding the correct word
   a. Describing using lots of "whatyamacallits" and "thingies"
   b. Common sayings come out slightly twisted

> I sometimes forget what I'm attempting to say and sometimes mangle metaphors and cliches....you can lead a horse where and then do what with it? (Schultz, 2011)

6. Trouble with math
   a. Memorizing multiplication facts

> When Douglas Merrill was young, he struggled to make basic academic connections. As he told us, "Every summer my mother was reteaching me to add, subtract, multiply, and divide all the way up till I was in college...Math never clicked for me. (Eide, 2011)

b. Sequencing of steps

> Now, as we approach the end of her senior year, *Kenlee* has finally shared with us that when she reads, letters look the same or get mixed up. She still struggles with math because she mixes the order of operations. *Kenlee* said she never told her dad and I about the letters and numbers because that's the way it has always been and 'I knew I was just stupid.' (Parent)

c. Directionality

> She had a lot of frustration working addition and subtraction problems (because) she wanted to work them from left to right. (Parent)

d. Telling time with a clock with hands

7. Dreads going to school

> He does not enjoy school, except recess. (Parent)

a. Complains of stomach aches or headaches

> The stress of dealing with school is giving him headaches, sleeplessness, and seems to be causing him to shut down. (Parent)

> She started making all kinds of excuses because she didn't want to go to school. She was sick, she had a headache, she had a stomachache. (Voncille Wright as quoted in Hubbell, 2012)

b. May drop out of high school

> *Kenlee* has a very deep hole to climb out of in order to graduate…She states, "I'm just done Mom, just done."…. She likes the on-line classes because the computer will read to her….I questioned how she has gotten to her senior year and no one other than the one math teacher noticed there was something going on with this kid….The school officials said that there were never any indicators of a learning issue, with their strongest defense, state assessments. *Kenlee* passed the tests, so there were never any red flags. (Parent)

8. Extremely messy bedroom, backpack, and desk

Adults

Education history similar to above, plus:

1. Slow reader
2. Having to read a page 2 or 3 times to understand it
3. Terrible speller
4. Difficulty putting thoughts onto paper
5. Continued difficulties with right versus left
6. Often gets lost, even in a familiar city

While these indicators are important when trying to identify dyslexia, each indicator is like looking at an individual puzzle piece. The puzzle cannot be completed unless we add the pieces that indicate strengths and personality traits. No individual should be identified by weaknesses alone. When we recognize all the pieces that make up an individual's inner makings, then the pieces can be fit together to become a beautiful masterpiece. Blake Charlton, a med student and novelist, who happens to be dyslexic, speaks to the importance of looking at the whole individual in *Defining My Dyslexia (nytimes.com/2013).*

I believe that scientific evidence and social observation will continue to show that defining dyslexia based solely on its weaknesses is inaccurate and unjust, and places too grim a burden on young people receiving the diagnosis. A more precise definition of dyslexia would clearly identify the disabilities that go along with it, while recognizing the associated abilities as well. If the dyslexic community could popularize such a definition, then newly diagnosed dyslexics would realize that they, like everyone else, will face their futures with a range of strengths and weaknesses. (Blake Charlton)

Nelsan Ellis describes the reading process like trying to put together a puzzle, but doing so with pieces that just didn't fit together. In our schools, we try to teach students with just half of the puzzle pieces. We have a good grasp of the weakness pieces; we tend to ignore the strength pieces. Is it any wonder many of our students rebel, shut down, and climb into a hole of depression?

Myth: People with dyslexia see backwards.
Busted:

> Dyslexics do not see things backwards because dyslexia is not a problem with the eyes. (DyslexiaHelp, *Debunking the Myths*; www.dyslexiahelp.umich.edu)

> One of the most enduring misconceptions is that dyslexic children see letters and words backward. (Shaywitz, 2003)

3

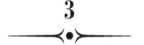

? Late Bloomer ?

Learning Differences that Require

Instructional Change

Cooper's Story: First Pants, Then Shoes!

Cooper leapt excitedly across the room, his face beaming with pride. After shutting himself off from the world for three days, with a keep out sign posted on the door, he was overjoyed to finally be done with his autobiography. All the hard work was behind him as he waved two sheets of paper, dripping with glue, at his mom. *No words?* Jeanine thought as she looked at the collage of cartoons plastered all over the two pieces of paper. Looking over this unexpected result of her son's intense work, she thought, *What was he doing in there all this time?* and *Would any fifth grade teacher really accept this?* Jeanine kept these thoughts to herself as she put on a face of pride.

After a closer look at the assignment Cooper held up so proudly, Jeanine was able to see the deep thought he had put into it. Her son's personality was actually depicted in the carefully chosen *Far Side* cartoons, and he had managed to paint a picture of who he was, using several Gary Larson illustrations. Cooper captured not only how he thinks but also how many with dyslexia think.

His autobiography demonstrated that he had a better grasp of himself than the average fifth grader. The cartoons he chose depicted his ability to laugh at himself, as well as using a healthy sense of humor to cope with the daily frustrations. In addition to capturing the value of humor in his life, he recognized several important traits about himself.

He recognized himself in an illustration of a spider saying, *"That CAN'T be right!"* while surveying his finished, but tangled web; the same bewildered look Cooper often had after completing written work. He also demonstrated a deeper understanding of himself when seeing himself in the cartoon entitled "First pants, then shoes!" sprawled across a young boy's wall as he gets out of bed. He had to admit he had difficulty with sequencing, with a tendency to act first then think, similar to the boy's need for a reminder of steps for dressing. As Cooper perused through *The Far*

Side Gallery, he found himself especially drawn to the cartoons picturing practical jokes or creative ideas gone wrong, a predicament he frequently found himself in. Science has opened the door of knowledge to dyslexia, and Cooper was able to capture some key aspects of how it affected his life.

"The dyslexic's ability to think is based on movement and energy, not on language expression," Jeanine explains. This unique way of thinking, based in movement instead of words, are characteristics shared by Albert Einstein, as we see by his analysis of how he processes information: "The words of the language, as they are written or spoken, do not seem to play any role in my mechanism of thought." Jeanine continues to explain that many with dyslexia don't have that internal conversation that so many of us carry around in our heads. When many of us get up in the morning, we start thinking and planning our day, asking ourselves if and what we'll eat for breakfast, what we'll wear, and the self-talk goes on throughout the day. In Cooper's world, he gets up and just goes with no thought of what's next.

Cooper's creative autobiography was just one of many incidents throughout his schooling when he had to learn to problem-solve in order to survive. As early as his kindergarten year, he discovered challenges. Cooper would come home from school saying his teacher was mean to him. Day after day, he stated that his teacher didn't like him, so Jeanine decided to pursue the issue. An informal conference resulted in a dead end, with the request to give her son some occasional encouragement falling on deaf ears. The teacher stated that she would not give preferential treatment to any student, including Cooper. Jeanine felt like she and her son were just brushed off and, in retrospect, wishes she would have pulled him out of that class. After all, kindergarten sets the stage for the remainder of a child's school career, and in order to get a good jumpstart, children must have positive strokes.

In our schools, it is very common to attribute the struggles that some kindergarteners and first graders experience to just being "late bloomers." However, Cooper's first grade teacher did not think this was the case for him. In fact, early in the school year she told Jeanine that in her thirty-five years of teaching, she hadn't seen anyone so smart that she couldn't teach to read. This was one of those teachers who cared deeply about her students and their success, and her concern led to saying, "If I were you I'd run to an educational psychologist." That is exactly what Jeanine did, and Cooper was given a diagnosis of profound dyslexia.

Cooper had two important things going for him that made huge impacts on his life. He had an advocate for a mother, and he was a risk-taker who wouldn't give up. While being willing to take risks and not giving up in the face of failure are traits that would ultimately lead to success, it also created worry for his parents. His daredevil personality earned him the nickname of tree boy because he would climb above the branches of trees in order to feel the wind and see better. Just like he could get a bird's eye view when climbing trees, he had the ability to see the big picture or grasp concepts with deep understanding, a strength that made many wonder why he struggled with the basic skills of reading and writing. Cooper's drive and energy led to an exceptional athletic ability, which brought a much-needed outlet in school. Put this with being a risk-taker who wouldn't give up, and you have the recipe for success no matter what one faces.

Having a parent advocate is another key factor that took Cooper further than what initial school experiences thought possible. Jeanine's own personal experiences with dyslexia motivated her to do whatever it would take, a journey that would change the course of her own life as well as her son's. The last thing she wanted was for him to have to go through the difficulties that she had endured. When learning that Cooper was profoundly dyslexic and realizing that schools were still not equipped to help those with dyslexia, she made the commitment to get the training needed to teach her son. This meant repeated trips to Texas to become certified to teach the Orton-Gillingham approach, using the Alphabetic Phonics Program. Cooper was in the first grade when Jeanine began working with him, using the information gained so far. Fortunately, the teacher who told

Jeanine to "run to an educational psychologist" also made it possible for her to tutor him in the mornings when he was fresh. The one-on-one intervention was tailored to her son's needs, and was done in place of the regular language arts curriculum. Trips to complete the coursework continued through the next five years, and tutoring continued until he was in the fifth grade. Ultimately, Jeanine became a qualified instructor for the Academic Language Association.

Cooper's official diagnosis of profound dyslexia brought the understanding that the therapy needed would be extensive and time-consuming. No quick fixes even though there are many claims to easier routes. Desperate families are searching the Internet and grasping at straws to try to get the answers to their child's struggles in the classroom. This desperation becomes amplified when they realize educators are also scratching their heads as to how to teach those with dyslexia. Jeanine and Cooper even tried some of these techniques and strategies that claim to help those with dyslexia.

One of the more common strategies that claims to help those with dyslexia is visual tracking therapy. Cooper tried this for six weeks with no signs of it making a positive impact. He also tried the use of colored overlays when reading, which brought no improvement in Cooper's reading. Another strategy that claims to improve working memory and ADHD, through brain/body integration, involves exercises done with balls to promote cross hemisphere motor and brain development. Cooper worked with a chiropractor who put together a program for him with the hope that the juggling exercises would help alleviate his reading disabilities. The benefit it did have for Cooper was learning to juggle well enough to win a talent show during Spirit Week, and of course, it was fun for awhile. Unfortunately, none of these strategies had any effect on Cooper's ability to read and write.

But there is good news for Cooper. He made remarkable improvement despite being profoundly dyslexic, and the credit is due to five years of intense specialized instruction. Many with dyslexia *need* this kind of intensive training; benefits rarely come from quick fixes for those who have dyslexia to this degree.

Cooper recently earned his bachelor's degree in biology and chemistry from Wichita State University after one final battle with academia. Despite the fact that he was now able to complete college-level coursework, dyslexia is never outgrown, and its effects are felt lifelong. It was his drive, energy, and inquisitive nature that carried him through the challenging college coursework, and even that almost wasn't enough. He came very close to not graduating despite his hard work. He had the legal documents that exempted him from having to take three semesters of a foreign language, but it was ignored until the issue was pushed. These legal documents were in the form of a 504

Plan, which is one avenue through which students with learning disabilities can receive accommodations. These documents gave Cooper the right to exemption of nonessential classes: three semesters of foreign language. More information on obtaining 504 plans will be in chapter 8, *The Importance of Advocacy.*

Although it is good for students to learn to advocate for themselves, sometimes they need someone with more experience; someone who knows how to climb up the chain of command until getting answers and results. This was the case for Cooper. Jeanine again went to bat for her son, which took climbing to the senior academic administrator. They again had to educate the college institution on the rights allowed through a 504 Plan and the discriminatory implications when these rights are not met. With persistence, Cooper's plan was followed, and he graduated with a dual degree.

Cooper and his mother share more than just the diagnosis of dyslexia. They both have an inner drive and perseverance that defies all odds. When they put their minds to meeting a particular goal or righting an injustice, there is no stopping them. The ability to problem-solve, often in an outside-the-box type of thinking, makes reaching goals achievable. Cooper's creative version of an autobiography, when in the fifth grade, was just one of many instances when difficult tasks were mastered. Add an insatiable energy to his other traits, and you have the assurance of great accomplishments.

What Works?

> Factors that lead to success: First, early in the child's life, someone has been extremely supportive and encouraging. Second, the young dyslexic found an area in which he or she could succeed. Finally, successful dyslexics appear to have developed a commitment to helping others. (International Dyslexia Association)

Take an imaginary trip with me for a moment. Imagine for a moment that one of your loved ones, who is typically full of life and energy, suddenly falls ill. You think it might just be the flu, but the sickness hangs on and on and on, leaving them unable to enjoy life, exhausted, and depressed. What would you do? I imagine you would do whatever was in your power to find out why they were sick and what could be done to bring them back to health and happiness.

Likewise, the student who wonders why he isn't learning like his classmates is often exhausted and depressed, similar to someone with an ongoing illness. And just like we would go to great lengths to help someone who is ill, shouldn't we do the same for the child suffering in the classroom? Especially if some of the suffering can be alleviated.

So let's get down to the nuts and bolts of what works and see if we can turn things around for these misunderstood children. Knowledge is necessary for all, not just educators. If we are going to be successful at making much-needed changes to benefit those with dyslexia, we need everyone's voice.

There are four key aspects that are necessary, or at the minimum helpful, when working with those with dyslexia. They are appropriate remediation, early intervention, qualified teachers, and respect, understanding, and patience for the student. Although having the benefit of all four would impact the individual with dyslexia to a greater degree, each aspect has its own unique benefits.

I. APPROPRIATE REMEDIATION

There are many forms of remediation, but there is only one method that has research-based evidence dating back to the 1930s. It is referred to as the Orton-Gillingham approach, and has had a profound impact in the lives of many with dyslexia.

What is the Orton-Gillingham Approach?

The Orton-Gillingham Approach, referred to as O-G throughout the remainder of this chapter, is an instructional approach intended primarily for those with dyslexia, but beneficial for anyone who has difficulty with reading, spelling, and writing. It is language-based, multisensory, structured, sequential, cumulative, cognitive, and flexible. It is very different from the curriculum used in many of our classrooms because it allows for a more individualized, flexible pacing with more opportunities for tapping into each student's dominant learning style.

In the 1930s, neurologist Dr. Samuel T. Orton and educator-psychologist Anna Gillingham developed the Orton-Gillingham (O-G) approach to reading instruction. There are numerous programs today that incorporate methods and principles first described in their foundational work, as well as other practices supported by research. Research has reinforced the value of an explicit, structured approach to teaching letter-sound relationships, syllable patterns, meaningful word parts, and language as a whole, for all students, especially those with dyslexia.

Lives can be turned around for the lucky students who receive instruction using an O-G program. Not only do numerous studies attest to this, but many parents and students have verified the positive impact of appropriate teaching methods.

> Then I found the International Dyslexia Association, and through the IDA I found The Kildonan School. After six weeks of summer camp there, my son told

us that he learned more than he had in his whole
life. They used Orton-Gillingham methods, and
that's what worked. (Diana Naples as quoted in
Hubbell, 2012)

A closer look at some of the distinguishing features
that makes up a comprehensive program may bring clarity.
Extensive research has demonstrated that a good language-
based program will combine O-G teaching approaches
with the five components of reading instruction as outlined
by the National Reading Panel Report. In 1997, Congress
asked the National Institute of Child Health and Human
Development (NICHD) to work with the US Department
of Education to establish the reading panel to evaluate
existing research and evidence to find the best ways to teach
children to read. The report came from a fourteen-member
panel made up of school administrators, working teachers,
and scientists involved in reading research. They completed
their study in 2003, at which time, the five components
were released in a report. The following is a breakdown of
features of the O-G approach and the five components
of reading instruction: when combined, they make a solid
language-based program.

<u>Orton-Gillingham Approach</u>	<u>Five Components of Reading Instruction</u>
Multisensory	Phonological Awareness
Phonics	Phonics
Personalized, Diagnostic, and Prescriptive	Fluency
Direct Instruction, Systematic, and Sequential	Vocabulary
Applied Linguistics	Comprehension

Multisensory

Multisensory teaching approaches typically incorporate three learning pathways: auditory, kinesthetic, and visual. Incorporating taste and smell when it can further reinforce a concept is an added bonus. For example, there are many food names that end in 'consonant-*le*' (final stable syllables), and students love the assignment of looking for other foods that follow the same pattern. Some of my students' favorites were:

- Apple—final stable syllable, *ple*
- Skittles—final stable syllable, *tle* and suffix, *s*
- Fiddle Faddle—final stable syllable, *dle*

After introducing the sound, discovering the visual, or how the sound is spelled, students incorporate tactile, and sometimes smell and taste while guessing the item tucked away in the guessing bag. This activity can be implemented in a large group setting as well as with individuals or small groups. Multisensory methods are more likely to tap into a student's dominant learning style, and therefore more likely to stick.

Visual and kinesthetic reinforcement is used by encouraging students to see and feel how sounds are formed with their mouth, using small mirrors, and feeling if the sound is voiced or unvoiced. Another kinesthetic practice that incorporates the entire body is skywriting. Reading and writing are taught simultaneously through an intricate routine of introducing sounds then discovering and writing the associated letter combinations. Skywriting is the process of leading a student to write the letter(s) in the air.

Phonics

Phonics is the study of letter sounds, syllables, word parts, and meaning parts, which are called morphemes: prefixes, suffixes, Latin roots, and so on. The teaching of phonics is critical to those who have weak rote memory skills, common to those with dyslexia. Learning to read by relying on memorization is a huge source of frustration for many.

Phonics moves beyond individual sounds, or phonemes, to syllable instruction. There are only six syllable types, and once students learn those, and the procedure for syllable division, they can decode at least 80 percent of the words in our language. Similarly, once they learn the forty-four sounds in the English language and the spelling patterns and rules, they can read and spell 85 percent of the words in our language.

Phonics is incorporated into some reading curriculum used in schools although it is often presented in a haphazard way with little to no review of previously learned concepts, which is necessary for most dyslexics. It is usually a suggested add-on to programs, and up to individual school districts if it is implemented. The days of teachers having the freedom to teach in an individualized manner and structuring what they teach to the needs in their classroom has been replaced with being told what and how to teach. Plus, teaching approximately thirty children makes it almost impossible to reach the whole gamut of ability levels.

The study of phonics goes beyond decoding sounds and words. It takes the phonic rules and transfers them to writing: first sounds, then words, then phrases. All students, especially those with dyslexia, benefit from being taught reading, spelling, and writing as a cohesive unit, and it should be explicit and based on rules.

Personalized, Diagnostic, and Prescriptive

Individuals with dyslexia vary greatly in their language and academic needs, their need for individualized pacing, and their learning styles. For example, it is common for dyslexics to have attention deficit disorder (ADD) or attention deficit disorder with hyperactivity (ADHD) and consideration of this should influence the style of teaching. Instruction and pacing are tailored to each individual. The pace and the degree of difficulty of the reading materials used are determined by the individual student's level of ability.

Likewise, to be diagnostic and prescriptive, lessons should reflect continuous monitoring of the student's progress. Just like a doctor evaluates the needs of the patient, prescribing medicines, therapy, and other resolutions to health issues, the teacher or therapist determines what instructional elements the student needs to focus on. This should be determined by looking at areas of weakness while using methods that provide opportunities to use strengths. Previous lessons drive the planning process as progress is monitored on a continuous basis.

Direct Instruction, Systematic and Sequential

All of the components of the Orton-Gillingham approach, from phonics to reading, spelling, and written language, are presented to students in a very systematic and sequential order. Concepts are presented from easiest and most commonly used to more complex and least used. This helps students experience success and confidence as they move through the program.

Some children can remember a concept that is taught, whether it is a letter name or sound, a letter combination, or a word, after only a few exposures, but others need repeated exposures. The average child needs between four and fourteen exposures to recognize a letter, sound, or word automatically; a dyslexic child often needs thousands of exposures. The techniques used to introduce new concepts offer multiple repetitions through use of multisensory strategies, plus review of previously learned concepts are built into the daily routines. Since the brain is highly reprogrammable, the routines can gradually alter the way the brain processes information.

Applied Linguistics

In today's classroom, we often try to separate reading instruction from written language. However, an emphasis with the O-G approach is to incorporate reading, spelling, and writing together. For example, learning individual sounds involves both reading and spelling of the sound. Students progress through the patterns of language: syllables, morphemes (a word or part of a word that has meaning), phrases, and sentences, including the grammatical structures of language and our writing system. Written language begins at an oral level until students are ready to progress to sentence structure and recognition of common literary forms used by writers.

Phonological Awareness

Phonological awareness is the ability to hear sounds that make up words in spoken language. This includes recognizing words that rhyme, distinguishing initial, medial, and final sounds in words, deciding whether words begin or end with the same sounds, understanding that sounds can be manipulated to create new words, and segmenting phonemes, syllables, and words within sentences.

Phonics and phonological awareness are often thought of as the same even though they are very distinct in their use of sensory input. Phonics starts with the visual and connects the print (letter combinations) to their sound, requiring the use of eyes and ears; phonological awareness is the awareness of sounds only, void of the print, requiring the use of ears only.

Dr. G. Reid Lyon has thirty years of experience as a public school educator, professor, research scientist, psychologist, and policymaker. He presented pertinent information in an *Overview of Reading and Literacy Initiatives* to the

Committee on Labor and Human Resources, Washington DC, in 1998. In Dr. Reid Lyon's report he tells us that children need phonological awareness and phonics to be taught directly and explicitly.

> Strong evidence that it is not the ear that understands that a spoken word like "cat" is divided into three sounds and that these discrete sounds can be linked to the letters C-A-T, it is the brain that performs this function. In some youngsters, the brain seems to have an easy time processing this type of information. However, in many children, the skill is only learned with difficulty, and thus must be taught directly, explicitly, and by a well-trained and informed teacher. Does this mean that children who have difficulty understanding that spoken words are composed of discrete individual sounds that can be linked to letters suffer from brain dysfunction or damage? Not at all. It simply means that the neural systems that perceive the phonemes in our language are less efficient than in other children. (Dr. Reid Lyon)

Fluency

Reading fluency comes with practice, and when a student does not like to read because it is difficult, they don't get the practice they need. Even after getting the right help by a qualified teacher, individuals with dyslexia often continue to read slowly. Dyslexia is not outgrown; the correct remediation helps them to learn strategies that can make it easier, but many aspects of dyslexia do not totally go away. This is especially the case with increasing the rate or speed of reading.

Despite the possibility that reading fluency may never be a strength, it needs to be regularly practiced and therefore is a regular component of good language programs. In the beginning stages, students work on rapidly naming letter names and sounds, working their way up to words, phrases, and passages that follow patterns they've learned.

Reading with fluency does increase a student's ability to comprehend and therefore reading at a slow rate can have a negative effect on comprehension, especially with pulling out the finer details of what they've read. On the other hand, even when students read at a slow rate, they often get the main idea, or they get the *gist* of what they read. I have been amazed at some of my students' knack for just getting it, after barely being able to read a passage; whereas others who read fluently sometimes are oblivious of what they just read.

> As one child recently remarked, "if you don't ride a bike fast enough, you fall off". Likewise, if the

reader does not recognize words quickly enough, the meaning will be lost. (Dr. G. Reid Lyon)

Vocabulary and Comprehension

Students with dyslexia benefit from the incorporation of activities that build vocabulary and comprehension skills. Many students with dyslexia have strong vocabulary and comprehension skills, however, struggling with reading the text can interfere with these skills.

When students struggle with decoding words and therefore have a slow fluency rate, comprehension can be lost in the process. All of the brain's energy is focused on reading the words, so recalling what they read suffers. Likewise, if students are frustrated with the difficult process of reading, they aren't as likely to pick up books to read, and limited reading leads to less exposure to new vocabulary.

New vocabulary words can be taught by having the student create their own vocabulary notebook, but instead of using definitions with words, they can use their creative juices to draw out a depiction of the word's meaning. With some action words, such as verbs or adverbs, they can be used in a game of Charades, and nouns and adjectives, can be used in Pictionary.

Comprehension activities can include diagramming the story, using graphic organizers, acting it out, and paraphrasing it. Students can be encouraged to give a quick recap of what they have read by using the five question words— WHO, WHAT, WHEN, WHERE, and WHY.

Comprehension is usually stronger for dyslexic students when they are read to or have access to text in audio versions. If the skill of decoding words, and eventually reading fluency, were taught as a separate subject from comprehension skills, we would often find the hidden strengths of those with dyslexia. When the student with dyslexia is free from the struggles of print, and they are given access to audio versions of text, they often soar. Separating the skills of decoding and comprehension would give us a more accurate assessment of a student's overall abilities and would give much-needed encouragement to the student who faces daily reminders of what he *can't* do.

Research That Supports

Why are our schools dragging their feet when it comes to implementation of the right remediation for our dyslexic students? It is especially puzzling when numerous studies have demonstrated success of programs that incorporate Orton-Gillingham methodology and the five components outlined by the National Reading Panel. The number of studies are too numerous for this book, but the following two studies are representative of many others that have resulted in similar growth after students were taught using an O-G program.

Many studies have demonstrated approximately two years of growth after a year of using a good language-based program that incorporates the elements listed above. Below are two examples: one group of participants had dyslexia, and the other group included students who qualified for special education services, which typically would encompass a wide variety of disabilities.

Orton-Gillingham Remediation Studies

	West Virginia Special Education Study	Alaska Dyslexia Study
Participants	6 Special education students in 4th-6th grades	45 Dyslexic Students in 2nd–11th grades
# of hours / week for Remediation	90 min. / week	Elementary: 2-3 hrs./week High School: 5 hrs./week
Total Length of Remediation	1 Year	6 months
Average years of Growth	2 Years Growth	2 Years Growth

(Bright Solutons for Dyslexia: http://dys-add.com)

Alphabetic Phonics is the program I was trained to use, and continue to use with students. It is considered a comprehensive program because it incorporates all of the elements of the Orton-Gillingham approach and the five components of reading instruction. There are other comprehensive programs, and where you live often determines which programs are readily available to you as noted by a past president of the Orton Society.

> Dr. Orton worked with Anna Gillingham, a school psychologist, and Bessie Stillman, an educator, to develop a structured language program now called the Orton-Gillingham Method. Its great success has bred many offshoots and has created a lot of sibling rivalry. Now we have the Slingerland Institute, mostly on the West Coast. We have Project Read in the Great Lakes area. We've got Alphabetic Phonics, down in Texas primarily. We've got Spalding, which is based in Arizona and is widely used in the Southwest. And then there is the Wilson Language System, based in New England. I am probably missing some more, but they are all wonderfully effective methods that have been derived from Orton and Gillingham. (Sylvia O. Richardson, MD as quoted in Hubbell, 2012)

As Dr. Richardson states, there are other good programs, and some fit the requirements to be a comprehensive program. There are also other good and helpful programs that only incorporate the O-G approach, and therefore reading and writing instruction needs to extend beyond that particular program. When you are looking at possible remediation programs, it is important to determine which elements are incorporated. Does the program use multisensory methods? Does it allow for personalization, using systematic and sequential direct instruction? Does it include phonological awareness and phonics instruction? Does it incorporate fluency practice? Are there vocabulary and comprehension activities? It is critical that remediation includes all the components in order to be considered a comprehensive language program.

II. Early Intervention

The importance of early intervention is confirmed by two long-term studies done by Connie Juel in 1988 and Cunningham and Stanovich in 1997. Their research predicted reading achievement based on how well they did in the first grade. A poor reader in the first grade was almost certain to remain a poor reader. Additional research shows that students at risk for reading failure can be easily identified when they are in kindergarten using phonological awareness tests. If they are given intensive, explicit instruction in phonological awareness and phonics in kindergarten through first grades, the need for remediation later is considerably less likely.

> Early intervention is so critical because it is about not wasting time. But more importantly, it's about taking advantage of the incredible plasticity of the brain–the ability of the brain to change under different environmental conditions. That plasticity is at really high levels from birth up to the age of eight or so, and that is when we need to make sure we're identifying and remediating dyslexia. Actually, the best time to identify is at kindergarten or before. If you wait, plasticity is reduced, so remediation is going to take longer and be more frustrating. (Gordon Sherman, PhD as quoted in Hubbell, 2012)

Dr. G. Reid Lyon's report tells us of the benefits of both phonological awareness and phonics instruction; he also includes statistics demonstrating the importance of early intervention.

> Phonemic awareness skills assessed in kindergarten and first grade serve as potent predictors of difficulties learning to read. We have learned how to measure phonemic awareness skills as early as the first semester in kindergarten with tasks that take only 15

minutes to administer–and over the past decade we have refined these tasks so that we can predict with approximately 80% to 90% accuracy who become good readers and who will have difficulties learning to read. We have learned that for 90% to 95% of poor readers, prevention and early intervention programs that combine instruction in phoneme awareness, phonics, fluency development, and reading comprehension strategies, provided by well trained teachers, can increase reading skills to average reading levels.

However, we have also learned that if we delay intervention until nine-years-of-age, (the time that most children with reading difficulties receive services), approximately 75% of the children will continue to have difficulties learning to read throughout high school. To be clear, while older children and adults can be taught to read, the time and expense of doing so is enormous. (Dr. G. Reid Lyon)

As more brain research is being produced, there is evidence of children's brains being very pliable, capable of tremendous amounts of learning and change, especially early in their lives. Some parts of our world are tapping into this strong evidence more than others. Students from Finland are benefiting from their schools taking action. In 2000, Finland became known for having the best young readers in the world, according to the Programme for International Student Assessment (PISA). By 2003, they led in math, and by 2006, they were first out of fifty-seven countries in science. Their success is contributed to small schools and classroom sizes where teachers know every student and a collaboration and consultation system that allows teachers to keep searching for strategies until something works for each individual student. According to the article "Why are Finland's Schools Successful?" (Smithsonian.com), "Nearly 30 percent of Finland's children receive some kind of special help during their first nine years of school. We try to catch the weak students. It's deep in our thinking." Their "whatever it takes" attitude continues to drive them.

Currently the Finnish government is investing money and time into how to help dyslexic children, with an emphasis on how to turn them around before they are in the first grade. Dr. Tomi Guttorm, from the University of Jyvaskyla in Finland, has spent ten years studying dyslexia and he sees it as a specific problem that can have a profound effect if children are not helped early.

When dyslexia is not found and treated early, it tends to snowball. As children get more and more behind in school, they often become increasingly frustrated, feeling like a failure. Often, self-esteem problems lead to negative behavior and other problems.

The mounting evidence that points to the importance of early intervention is disregarded in many schools, resulting in lives being unnecessarily damaged. Diana King attests to the fact that we have known for some time that children's lives can be turned around when they receive intervention early. She recalls when Anna Gillingham came into the school where she taught. After screening kindergarteners, Gillingham placed those at risk in a first grade classroom that totally used the Orton-Gillingham approach. These children stayed together and continued with the same program until the end of fourth grade. At this time, the students were tested again, and she found that they had caught up with their peers, and they were better than their peers in spelling. On top of this, these children never had to fail and suffer the stigma of thinking they were stupid. The fact that this was in 1951 or '52 tells us that we've known how to fix these problems for a long time.

When identifying and treating dyslexia early, children are much more likely to reach their potential. In chapter 8, we will talk about the importance of advocating for our children, and this role has to start early if we want the best for our children.

> You can't wait and hope things get better. You can't listen to people who say, "Let's wait six months or a year, and it'll probably clear up." That's wasted,

wasted time. (Gordon Sherman, PhD as quoted in Hubbell, 2012)

III. QUALIFIED TEACHERS

Now, is the problem dyslexia or dysteachia. We need to go back to the teaching colleges and make sure they are teaching teachers the most effective way for all students to learn to read. If it is too late for some-one out there in the field, we need to help teach-ers get certified in structured language programs through workshops, to help them understand that there is a very powerful way to teach reading, and it may not be the way they learned in college. (Gordon Sherman, PhD as quoted in Hubbell, 2012)

The National Reading Panel's release of the five com-ponents of a good reading program in 2003 became the cornerstone for schools in their search for the best read-ing programs. Word traveled quickly, and districts began reevaluating their current curriculum. This was valuable information, and the schools I taught in took the "big five" very seriously. We dove in with great enthusiasm. But just like diving into a swimming pool is the first step in the act of swimming, diving into the broad aspects of the "big five" is just the first step to reading instruction. Successfully teaching children to read is a much more daunting task than teaching them to swim. We strived to keep our heads above water while swimming around the buoyancy lifelines of the "big five." I can recall feeling like the students and I were sinking to the bottom of the pool, wondering if we would ever reach the surface. This sinking feeling lessened considerably after learning the valuable O-G techniques, which gave me application tools to carry out the "big five."

I share the fact that my students and I often experienced sinking feelings because I know the frustrations that many teachers are experiencing. Our nation's illiteracy problems will not go away until all teachers are trained in research-based strategies for all students, not just the middle-of-the-road child. One critical aspect of teacher training must be learning how to work with the one in five children who have dyslexia.

In the "Overview of Reading and Literacy Initiatives," Dr. G. Reid Lyon also discusses the inadequate preparation of teachers.

> The need for informed instruction for the millions of children with insufficient reading skills is an increasingly urgent problem. Unfortunately, several recent studies and surveys of teacher knowledge about reading development and difficulties indicate that many teachers are underprepared to teach

reading. Most teachers receive little formal instruction in reading development and disorders during either undergraduate and/or graduate studies, with the average teacher completing only two reading courses. Course work is superficial and typically unrelated to teaching practice; and the supervision of student teaching and practicum experiences is fragmentary and inconsistent. At present, motivated teachers are often left to obtain specific skills in teaching phonemic awareness, phonics, reading fluency, and comprehension on their own by seeking out workshops or specialized instructional manuals. In reading education, teachers are frequently presented with a "One Size Fits All" philosophy that emphasizes either a "whole language" or "phonics" orientation to instruction. (Dr. G. Reid Lyon)

Having the opportunity to receive appropriate training changed my attitude toward teaching and the students with whom I worked. The Fundamental Learning Center's proven and successful research-based instruction has made it the leading source of literacy instruction in Kansas. It is one of eighteen sites in the nation accredited by the International Multisensory Structured Language Education Council (IMSLEC). At these sites, there is intensive training for classroom teachers, reading specialists, and other educators in Literacy Intervention Specialist Preparation Programs.

> Quality teachers are the single greatest determinant of student achievement. Teacher education, ability and experience account for more variation in student achievement than all other factors. Knowing the subject matter, understanding how students learn, and practicing effective teaching methods translate into greater student achievement. Just like practitioners in other professions, teachers need the opportunity to deepen their knowledge and improve their skills through quality research-based professional development. (Fundamental Learning Center)

Some teachers have to use their own resources to get the training they need. However, in my experience, parents go above and beyond if they have the monetary means to help their struggling child. Parents are searching the Internet, talking to other parents, and seeking advice from their child's teacher, and their search can lead them down helpful paths or it can lead them toward a dead end. Accreditation and certification of instructional organizations has become an important catalyst for protecting the public from approaches that have no sound basis in research. The International Multisensory Structured Language

Education Council (IMSLEC), under the umbrella of the International Dyslexia Association, has grown out of the increasing search for strategies that work. Accredited organizations provide training that is based in research, with requirements that assure participants are taught how to teach, what needs to be taught, and why particular techniques are necessary. Going into this much depth requires more than just a few hours of training.

Even though this type of training takes time and commitment, it is worth it when you see the impact it can have in the lives of those struggling to learn through traditional methods. The dyslexic child's transformation from the downtrodden look of defeat to a beaming look of pride makes all the effort worthwhile.

IV. Respect, Understanding, and Patience for Student

So far we've looked at what works from the standpoint of the teacher, parent, or advocate. But what about the student's perspective? What do they say they need? In *The Dyslexic Advantage*, many now successful individuals with dyslexia were interviewed, and when asked what factors were critical for their emotional and professional success, their responses were summed up as follows:

These factors included tenacity; confidence; positive self-image; a realistic acceptance of the personal struggles and shortcomings associated with dyslexic learning challenges, but also a deliberate focusing on personal strengths and areas of special interest; supportive home and school environments; and a supportive network of friends.

Student success goes beyond academic strategies and programs. Interactions should be based in a healthy mutual respect. A greater understanding of our student's uniqueness, learning needs, and interests will be met with a much greater willingness to tackle the tough day-to-day tasks. This holds true for all students, but especially for those with any type of a learning disability.

A mistake many of us make, which actually makes matters worse, is pushing students to try to work at the pace of their classmates. Granted, some students need a little prodding, but for the student with dyslexia, this tactic often backfires. The pressure and stress this creates can not only cause them to shut down, but it can also lead to negative reactions, such as anger, resistant behavior, depression, and anxiety. These reactions will be discussed at greater lengths in chapter 6, but it's important that we recognize what happens when children are repeatedly given challenges they cannot meet. It triggers an increasing stress that actually negatively affects working memory, focus, and motivation.

> That's why keeping children in environments where they feel chronically stressed is emotionally harmful and educationally counterproductive. We place demands on them that they can't possibly meet, then react with astonishment when they become frustrated, anxious, inattentive, bored, depressed, unruly, or overactive. But this response is inevitable, and the fault is ours, not theirs. Children crave success, and it's in their nature to learn and grow. If they reject what we are offering them, that rejection is often a form of defense that they're using to avoid failure when they feel that success is impossible. (Eide, 2011)

When students feel respected, understood, and are treated with patience, they will usually go the extra mile. A stress-free environment nurtures creativity, problem-solving, and the desire to learn. Nurturing relationships should be as much a part of education as teaching subject matter.

> Teachers who build positive relationships with their students and who take the time to connect with them

in meaningful ways have found the key that opens
the door to influential teaching. (Laughlin, 2015)

Summary

Giving children appropriate remediation, early intervention, quality teachers, and providing them respect, understanding, and patience can be the ticket to student success. Finding solutions and having the fortitude to carry
out what is needed is not a quick, easy fix. The National
Institute of Child Health and Human Development
(NICHD) has looked at research programs, which have
studied over thirty-four thousand children and adults. The
research tells us that learning to read is a formidable challenge for approximately 60% of our nation's children, and
for at least 20% to 30% of these children, reading is one
of the most difficult tasks that they will have to master
throughout their educational careers.

We would be remiss if we were to disregard the 20% to
30%, especially now that there are strategies that have been
proven to work. Research also shows that 95% of reading
failure is preventable by using appropriate reading systems
and well-trained teachers. So what are we waiting for!

Myth: He's just a late bloomer.
Busted:

> Students in the bottom 20% in basic reading skills are likely to be there for the duration of schooling unless something is done to help them overcome their problem. They do not spontaneously learn to read, and very few are late bloomers when it comes to reading.
>
> —Moats & Dakin (2008)

I started noticing *Kenlee* struggling with reading and writing in the 1st grade. I was told by her teacher it was something she would grow out of. By the 3rd & 4th grade I was requesting that testing be done to see if she needed special education....She did not qualify. Upon starting 6th grade she was failing almost every class, so I removed her from public school and started to homeschool. (Parent)

4

? There's No Dyslexia in our School ?
All Alike or Each Unique

Justin's Story: A Ray of Sunshine in
an Otherwise Miserable Day!

"Why are you going with THAT group?" "How come you leave every day?" "You're going with THEM?" These are some of the questions asked of Justin when he was pulled out of the classroom for small group help with reading and writing. The questions asked of this bright, articulate second grader made him feel embarrassed and different. He felt smart but conflicted, wondering why he wasn't able to read and write like his classmates.

I was the one who pulled him out of the classroom, along with four of his classmates. Justin became one of my biggest challenges academically yet his "little adult" vocabulary and his ability to "just get it" with more complex concepts drew me instantly to him. Plus, his wit and sense of humor broke through the monotony of school that brought much-needed laughter. In retrospect, he and I were usually the only ones laughing since the others usually didn't get it. He was able to see the forest even though he couldn't see the individual trees. In other words, he had common sense and the intelligence that made it possible for him to see the big picture despite not having the ability to perform what's considered the basic functions of reading and writing.

When we started working together, Justin was in the second grade, he was not reading yet, and his writing was illegible. He would do anything to get out of these difficult tasks. He was quite the talker and tried desperately to take us down a rabbit hole in order to dodge embarrassment or just avoid the task. I must admit sometimes he was successful. He could take us on some of the wildest "rabbit" chases. After all, it was often more interesting than the task at hand. I had to work very hard to make the mundane tasks interesting and engaging with activities that allowed him to use all his senses.

I was genuinely excited to work with this talkative, challenging group for more than just their personalities. It was my first opportunity to use the training I received at the Fundamental Learning Center with a group in a public school. Previously, I had tutored children outside of school, thus having more time to individualize to each student's strengths and weaknesses. In the school setting, time is more limited, and we rarely work with groups who have the same learning issues and needs. Typically, they are grouped by grade level, which was the case with this group.

Schools vary when it comes to allowing special education teachers the flexibility needed to adapt teaching strategies to individual student needs. Some districts limit teachers to use of specific curriculum. These are the districts, in my experience, that typically try to lump everyone into a one-size-fits-all package, denying that there is any student with dyslexia in their school. This was not the case in Justin's school. Fortunately, I was given the flexibility needed to use my newly acquired skills to teach several individuals, such as Justin. On the other hand, I was discouraged from calling dyslexia by its name; instead those with dyslexia were to be referred to as learning disabled.

Justin and the others responded well to the multisensory approach, as evidenced by the first question out of their mouths upon entering the room. "Do we get a guessing bag? Do we…. Do we?" The guessing bag activity was a fun way to use auditory and tactile senses to guess the object in the bag that matched one of the forty-four sounds of the English language. Their genuine excitement over the mystery object spurred me to create additional guessing games to help them discover new concepts that could be trans-ferred to learning to read and write.

With remediation it typically takes a minimum of two years to complete the Alphabetic Phonics program. Most require longer, especially if they are working in a small group with varying learning needs. That was the case for Justin. Catching up to his peers in reading finally happened after four to five years of intensive work. But even though he is now in honor classes in high school, anything involv-ing reading and writing are low on the totem pole for how Justin wants to spend his time. Reading fluently may never be easy; whereas his ability to comprehend will probably always exceed others.

In Justin's elementary years, reading was an agoniz-ingly slow process, not because he didn't *want* to read. He was actually working very hard. He was and still is smart enough to learn how to get good grades despite reading slowly. One thing he has always been good at is taking tests, even reading tests. After reading the text, which was a painstaking task for him, he comprehended both basic right-there questions as well as inference-type questions, which require higher level thinking skills.

When I asked Justin what kept him laughing and shrug-ging off the everyday struggle in the classroom, his response took me back to Justin in the second grade. His matter-of-fact answer was, "I'm ignorant!" What? This answer from a very confident, successful teenager! Anyone who spends time with those with dyslexia knows to question their word choices when they don't make sense. "Oh, I mean, I'm stubborn!" After a good laugh over just another language bobble, we talked about the common tendency to mix up words and phrases. The dyslexic brain's language processing differences goes much deeper than how print is perceived. Working with students and adults who have dyslexia has many perks beyond just their ability to think outside the box. Misquoting idioms and using words in the wrong context has brought much laughter over the years. Justin's teachers were often amazed at his use of vocabulary beyond his age, which made his language bobbles even more humorous.

Justin's description of himself as being stubborn, or as I would say, having perseverance, is key to his success. As Justin said, "I believe I can do it myself, and I get stubborn about believing this." This self-motivation led him and his family to decide to exit out of special education services and replace it with having accommodations through a 504 Plan (an explanation of 504 plans will be discussed in chapter 8). Justin's desire and drive to maneuver through school more independently played a big part in this decision. Plus he often felt that his classmates would "give him crap" when para educators would help him, often when Justin didn't think he needed it. He shared that he has his own unique pace that seems to be different from others, so when grouped with others that needed help, he felt "slowed down and not pushed enough."

Justin has some great advice for others who may find reading and writing difficult even though they know they are smart. Being in several honor classes in high school, a great deal of reading is required. He survives these tough classes by skimming over material in order to get the gist of the content, then decides what's important as he reads those sections with a "slow but steady" attitude. He shares that he likes opportunities to partner up because this makes it possible for him to get help with the reading and writing while helping his partners to see things they might not otherwise see. Problem-solving is just one of his many strengths. Also, his strong social skills make it possible to work well with everyone: "partnered with slackers or overachievers—we get 'er done." Classes that allow partnering up makes it possible for more individualization, which he sees as critical for all students' success.

He also shares another factor that takes him and often the whole class down a negative track—that is, boredom. One of his biggest pet peeves is having to do extra work because of other students' actions. He recalls having to complete a mundane dictionary assignment for no other purpose than punishment. He enjoys the classes that maintain a positive atmosphere, even if they require more work.

"You're a ray of sunshine in an otherwise miserable hour." This is what Justin's English literature teacher said to him after a particularly bad day. He has always been masterful at participating in classroom discussions. His ability to talk to anyone, no matter their age, and his strong leadership skills are strengths that do not go unnoticed. He has already earned his Eagle Badge in scouts and has been active in 4-H for most of his life. I still remember an essay he wrote about his best friend, Oreo, his cow, which he still has after seven years. The strong affection expressed as if Oreo were his household pet came through despite misspelling half of the words and handwriting that was just barely decipher-able. But the content made it a masterpiece! Athletic ability is another strong suit for Justin with football and baseball as favorites. A turn of events on the football field led him down a new pursuit. A football injury caused him to have to sit out for a time, which led to the opportunity to film games. Being behind the camera was just another hands-on job that he became quite skilled at.

When considering future endeavors, Justin has found that his industrial technology class has inspired him to want to create something from the designing process to actually making it. He doesn't have anything specific in mind, but as he said, if it's "something I enjoy, I will do the best I can at it." Justin already has a good grasp of who he is, and with his many strengths, his path forward is sure to be full of adventure and success!

Our Amazing Brains

The differences are personal, the diagnosis is clinical, the treatment is educational, the understanding is scientific.

—Margaret Byrd Rawson

"Wow! Look at that view!" I frequently hear something like this when my husband and I travel in the early fall season. As the highway paves its way through the gentle Kansas hills, I look up from the pages I'm reading to see only green where he is indicating. I used to ask, "Where?" I don't need to ask anymore because I know it's just how he perceives colors as compared to me. Yes, he is color bind, and it's been interesting for both of us to try to imagine what the other is seeing. He sees beauty in the varying shades of the same color, whereas I see the bright reds, yellows, and oranges of fall foliage as an amazing view. I've found that I can use our different ways of perceiving color as a means to shed light on differing ways of processing print.

Pulling out a picture of a stoplight, I begin with, "Can you believe my husband can't read this symbol! He has to remember that the top light means 'stop' and the bottom one means 'go,' and when the light is turned on its side, he has to be very careful to make sure he knows whether to go or stop. Red and green are the same to him." Their quizzical looks tell me they think there must be something wrong with him. I continue to tell them how smart he is, and in fact, in many ways I consider him smarter than me. After explaining that he is colorblind, I lead them into a discussion of our brain-processing differences. Just like the colorblind individual processes colors differently, the dyslexic brain processes letters, numbers, and words differently. And just like many intelligent people are colorblind, many intelligent people have dyslexia. By the time students come to me, their internal dialogue is already, *I'm stupid!* When encouragement is needed, I just pull out my stoplight as my way of reminding them that they are indeed smart.

As science is slowly opening the window into the brain, we must adjust our preconceived views of intelligence and the "this is the way we've always done it" type of thinking. Change is difficult but necessary. Some have already jumped on this bandwagon and are making huge impacts in the lives of children with dyslexia. But many are stuck like a cog in a wheel, relying on the old school thinking rather than looking at what studies are telling us about how our brains work. So what is brain research telling us about learning?

- The brain CAN change and reorganize
- Activation patterns in the brain determine strengths and weaknesses
- There are benefits and deficits to both right-brain dominance and left-brain dominance.

The Brain Can Change and Reorganize

In the last chapter, we discussed early intervention as one of the four key aspects needed to help the student with dyslexia reach their potential. Young children absorb new skills like a sponge because their brains are ready and pliable. Evidence tells us the brain is capable of reorganizing itself when given intensive remediation that lasts over an extended period of time. The result is a shift in brain response. This is evident when the imaging of fMRIs show the brain activation patterns prior to and after remediation.

Activation Patterns in the Brain Determine Strengths and Weaknesses

Drs. Sally and Bennett Shaywitz have been instrumental in bringing us concrete proof of how our brains influence our ability to perform academic skills, such as reading. In their studies, they have used functional magnetic resonance imaging (fMRI) to see the active parts of the brain as good readers and struggling readers perform this task.

> Dyslexia is neurobiological in origin with overwhelming and converging data from functional brain imaging investigations. The results of these studies suggest that there are observable differences in how the dyslexic brain functions when compared to the brain of a typical reader. (Shaywitz, 2003)

The imaging shows different activation patterns: the back portion stronger and the front weaker in the strong reader, and the front stronger and the back weaker when the dyslexic individual is reading. Shaywitz points out, "It is as if these struggling readers are using the systems in the front of the brain to try to compensate for the disruption in the back of the brain."

The complexity of our brain function goes beyond just the activation of the front and back parts of our brain; the activation patterns of the right and left hemispheres determine our learning styles and our strengths and weaknesses.

> The left hemisphere can recognize eyes and ears and noses and mouths, but it's poor at recognizing faces. Similarly, it can see windows and doors and chimneys and shingles, but it's poor at seeing houses. To

perceive these larger patterns, the left hemisphere requires big-picture processing help from the right. Individuals with dyslexia often show a distinctly 'right-brained style' or 'flavor' in the ways that they process information. Reading expert Dr. Maryanne Wolf summed up the results of this work by writing, "The dyslexic brain consistently employs more right-hemisphere structures for reading and its component processing activities than left-hemisphere structures. (Eide, 2011)

Thus, the struggle with the finer components of reading: recognizing abstract symbols of print. When tasks become more automatic and routine, the left side of the brain is primarily activated. Left-brain dominance leads to strengths in "tasks that require precision, accuracy, efficiency, speed, automaticity, focus, and detailed expertise," according to *The Dyslexic Advantage*. Right-side dominance, which is more prevalent in those with dyslexia, makes them more likely to "see the gist or essence of things or to spot the larger context behind a given situation or idea; multidimensionality of perspective; the ability to see new, unusual, or distant connections; inferential reasoning and ambiguity detection; the ability to recombine things in novel ways and a general inventiveness; and greater mindfulness and intentionality during tasks that others take for granted." The skills that require left-brain dominance—speed, automaticity, and focus, to name a few—are seen as important in the typical classroom. Skills that require right-brain dominance—inferential reasoning, multidimensional perspective, getting the gist of things, to name a few—are more important outside of the classroom in the real world.

In the classroom, the student who does not have the left-brain processing necessary for many of the basic academic tasks needs specialized help, and the earlier the better.

> Dr. Guinevere Eden and her colleagues at Georgetown University have shown that most beginning readers use both sides of their brain quite heavily—just like individuals with dyslexia. It's only with practice that most readers gradually shift to a largely left-sided processing circuit. Individuals with dyslexia have a much harder time making this shift to primarily left-sided, or "expert," processing. Without intensive training they tend to retain the "immature" or "beginner" pathway, with its heavy reliance on right-hemispheric processing. (Eide, 2011)

The Benefits and Deficits of Right-brain Dominance and Left-brain Dominance

Once we've mastered a task such as talking, walking, and even riding a bike, most of us can do it without even thinking about it. This ability is referred to as procedural learning. We take it for granted and enjoy these activities without hesitation. It is also referred to as unconscious or automatic memory, and flourishes when the left hemisphere of the brain becomes more activated. We unconsciously go about our days doing so many things that give us the independence we want, thanks to our wonderful brains.

Procedural learning is one of the challenges that many dyslexics face and is the reason why many of the rote tasks taught in schools are difficult. These rote tasks, especially in the early grades, are often very rule and procedure dependent, a weaker skill for those with dyslexia. The basic skills of reading and writing are taught using curriculum that assumes the student has automatic memory. But this is not the case for those with dyslexia, who learn better when tasks and skills are broken down into steps, clearly demonstrated and explicitly taught.

Students with procedural learning challenges also need more repetitions in order to master basic skills. They often can't retain these skills after only one or two exposures, making it necessary to review and practice what has already been taught. There are many good programs designed specifically for those who need to be taught in this manner, as discussed in the previous chapter.

Andrea, a mother of two dyslexic children, shared a beautiful analogy with me that helped her explain the need for tedious repetitions when teaching her children. Using this analogy helped motivate her children to persevere and push through the frustration.

> Imagine yourself on a beach watching the tide roll over repeatedly. Now, imagine taking a stick to draw a line in the sand, only to have the tide erase the indentation. So, you keep drawing that line, despite the water continuing to erase it. Finally, after persevering in your endeavor to create a mark, you begin to see that the water doesn't completely erase it, and the more times you draw that line, the deeper the crevice becomes. Likewise, with each repetition of a concept or task taught, it will become more imprinted in your brain, and eventually stick. (Andrea Hankins)

While it is true that the struggle with procedural learning can cause hardship for those with dyslexia, it also creates something positive. The flipside of the difficulty with automaticity in routine tasks is a greater creativity and problem solving ability. This right-brain dominance is not emphasized in the classroom, but it is seen as a great asset in the workforce. Many successful entrepreneurs, engineers, and architects, to name a few, achieved success because of these strengths, and their creativity is further strengthened by their difficulty with learning routine tasks. The weakness actually forces insight. They are forced to take on tasks with greater "mindfulness" because they have to really think about what they are doing. This encourages a creative and innovative way of approaching tasks, which can lead to finding better ways of doing them.

Summary

Once you know a student has these challenges and strengths, it changes how you look at them. They don't want nor need sympathy when they are struggling; rather, they need to be understood. And once they realize you appreciate and see their strengths, they are more likely to do the work needed to compensate for their weaknesses. British psychologist, Dr. Angela Fawcett, says, "Actually, the dyslexic child is working much harder than everybody else.... When you understand this, you realize that it's not something the child should be ashamed of, but something he should be taught to get around, using specific strategies."

Having an understanding of their strengths will encourage motivation to persevere through the challenges.

Our unique brains create diverse abilities from which we can all benefit. For example, in the Air Force there is a particular need for those who are colorblind. They need people who have red-green insensitivity because they are not fooled by camouflage when flying over enemy territory. Whether our brain processes color or print differently, there are tasks that require all types and variances.

> This is another part that fascinates me: dyslexics who are successful are often way out ahead of everybody else, and the teachers and the testers haven't a clue as to what they are talking about. Albert Einstein is a wonderful example of that. Very few people understood the kind of thing he was thinking about in 1903, but as he talked about his various theories of relativity, there were a few more people who began to understand, and now, in the field of telecommunications and satellites, these ideas are conventions of engineering, understood and used every day. It took us nearly a hundred years to catch up to what Albert Einstein was doing in his imagination. (Tom West as quoted in Hubbell, 2012)

The amazing power of the human brain can lead us in leaps and bounds beyond our imagination, and it starts with that struggling student in the classroom.

Myth: Dyslexia is rare.
Busted:

> Nationwide, 20% of the elementary school population is clearly struggling with reading, is at clear risk for academic failure, and is in need of remedial intervention or specialized instruction; that is, 1 child in 5, or at least 4 children per an average classroom of 20 children. (Moats & Dakin, 2008)

5

? Dyslexia = Vision Problem ?
Seeing Beyond Educational Traditions

Anna's Story: I Am Smart, I Just Learn Differently!

"What happened to Anna? She looks like a different girl?" The changes were evident to everyone. Anna had blossomed into a confident, happy girl. This dramatic change happened because, for the first time in Anna's life, she was with others like her who were smart despite the struggle to learn to read and write.

Anna's life was turned around mostly because of a change in schools. Her story has a happy ending, but early experiences in school were not so happy. Before beginning kindergarten, Anna was full of life and excited for school to begin. But the first year of school changed this happy child in a very visible way.

"You need to consider a special day class for Anna, because I'm not sure she's bright." Imagine the shock Anna's mother felt when hearing this kindergarten teacher's assessment of her creative, full-of-life daughter. If she had listened to this advice, Anna would be separated from her peers and placed in a special education classroom with students labeled as intellectually challenged. It is true that she was not picking up learning the alphabet and therefore was not learning to read like most of her classmates, but she was actually very bright. It was devastating to the family to have their daughter be so misunderstood, but the truth of Anna's capabilities would not be made evident to the public school system for eight years.

Fortunately for Anna, her family had already learned a great deal about dyslexia because of her older brother's experiences. When he struggled to learn to read, they were referred to an optometrist for vision therapy. Vision therapy is the most common recommendation for struggling readers because associating dyslexia with vision is one of the most prevailing myths. When vision therapy didn't work, they pursued tutoring services, which took him from being a nonreader to reading *Harry Potter* books in one year.

This was the hope for Anna when she began tutoring sessions; however, she did not respond as quickly. The family decided to take Anna to a specialist to seek advice. After an educational psychologist diagnosed her with dyslexia, Anna's developmental pediatrician told the family that although holding a child back is not the typical recommendation, in Anna's case she would make an exception. In light of Anna's negative first experience with school, perhaps a second go-round of kindergarten at a new school would give her the jump start she needed.

Anna continued with tutoring during her second kindergarten year, but during her first grade year her parents reluctantly agreed to stop the tutoring when the resource teacher strongly advised them to do so.

The next few years would become the trial period to see if she could make the progress needed to stay on the grade-level treadmill with her peers. However, Anna continued to struggle to learn through traditional methods in the classroom, and the family wondered if they had done the right thing. The reading resource teacher tried to assure them with promises to give her what she needed. "I can teach her how to read. I have a lot of tricks up my sleeve." Unfortunately these "tricks" did not work. During the summer months, the reading teacher would send home sight words and ask the family to help Anna memorize them. With weak rote memory skills, common to those with dyslexia, this strategy, or "trick," was amongst the trials that failed.

After two years of kindergarten and continuing through first and second grades, the family noticed the gap actually widening. In other words, her rate of progress was staying relatively the same while her peers' reading rates were at a steady incline. Teachers told them Anna was progressing, but the family saw little to no changes. In addition to this, and equally if not more important, she was enduring extensive bullying on the playground. Two of the more extreme incidents resulted in broken arms. On another occasion, Anna was pinned against a fence by the same girl who previously broke her arm, and when trying to escape, she scratched the bully's face. After a reprimand by the principal, her punishment was spelled out: Anna would spend the next recess writing an apology (for being bullied?), and she would write an additional paper telling how she could have handled the situation better. Defending herself resulted in punishments known to be extremely difficult for her.

Although they felt they had little control over the bullying, they could do something about the ever-widening gap. Anna's family decided to give tutoring a second chance. By this time, she was entering the third grade, reading at a kindergarten level and receiving no support for her dyslexia. Her frustration and defeated attitude had been building, and by the time she got home from school, she was exhausted and an emotional wreck. Her brain could take no more! So they decided to work with the teacher to find the best time possible to pull her out of school, a time when she would miss little to no academics. They worked around the classroom schedule so Anna would only miss lunch, recess, and the scheduled language arts time with the reading resource teacher. Instead, she would get her own individually specialized language program with her tutor. The only downfall was not being able to eat and play with her friends. This solution to a growing problem would ultimately lead to accusations of truancy.

But how did they get to the point of being labeled truant, a term often equated with neglectful parenting? Pursuing dyslexia remediation that took Anna out of the classroom was the trigger that got the legal ball rolling. When they started getting truancy notices, the family turned to an attorney for advice. After three notices, they had to appear before a truancy board. They answered the room full of board members, including an armed policeman, with a review of Anna's school history. With documentation in hand, they discussed Anna's struggles during her first years of education and the purpose of the tutoring, which included the improvements specialized instruction was bringing. She made approximately two years progress in reading in one year, which they directly attributed to the dyslexia remediation she received with tutoring. They countered the principal's claim that Anna was missing two hours of valuable instruction every day with the truth: she was only missing time in the resource room and instead getting the specialized help she needed.

The board backed the principal, despite several members showing obvious shock at the principal's actions, and asked the family to discontinue tutoring services during school hours. When the family did not agree to these terms, the board threatened prosecution by the district attorney. With the assurance that they were doing the right thing for their daughter, they willingly called the DA's office. After explaining their situation, they were told, "We would never prosecute you for that."

Throughout this time, Anna's frustration level was rising, and she repeatedly told her mom, "Everyone's smarter than me. I must be the dumbest person in the world." The decision to carry on with tutoring, despite the ongoing battle with the school, was extremely difficult but ultimately necessary. "Her first years of school were tragic, and to let her muddle through with increasing hits to her self-esteem was not an option."

In light of Anna's devastating school experiences and the board's actions, they filed against the school district. After unsuccessful attorney collaborations, mediation was the next step. By this time, Anna had finished third grade, and the family was enjoying a break from the stresses of school. Fortunately, mediations brought an agreement the family was okay with, but it also brought the realization that there would be no changes at the school Anna attended. Dyslexia remediation was nowhere in their realm of thinking.

Therefore, Anna made a second school change; she was enrolled in a private Christian school for her fourth grade year where there was a classroom for children with learning disabilities. A new school brought a more positive atmosphere, a welcome relief for the whole family.

While attending a private school was a welcome relief for Anna's fourth grade year, another possibility was brought to their attention during the summer before her fifth grade year. The family learned of Athena Academy, a school designed specifically for those with dyslexia. This would be the third change and the catalyst for a complete transformation. Prior school experiences had taken their toll on Anna's self-esteem, and when she first walked through Athena Academy's doors, her body language screamed that she didn't belong or have any value. She tried desperately to hide behind her hair, which hung over her eyes, and she walked hunched over, avoiding all eye contact. But this demeanor would not continue for long.

Athena Academy was the reason Anna's personality was changing before their eyes. It was her uncles who brought it to everyone's attention with, "What happened to Anna? She looks like a different girl?" It was evident that something was changing inside this wounded little girl. After six weeks, her transformation was like that of a butterfly learning it can fly. Finding others who learn like her and discovering that she is, indeed, intelligent changed her from the inside out. She embraced her new school's philosophy and realized, "I am smart! I just learn differently."

Anna is one of the lucky ones. Her family knew enough about dyslexia to take action. They took their roles of advocacy very seriously. Anna made such remarkable progress over the next two years that she is now back in a public school as a seventh grader and is fully mainstreamed in all classes. This was the fourth school change, and the bumpy road in between turned out to be worth it. The original assessment of being categorized as intellectually challenged had been proven wrong. She was learning with her peers, and getting all As and Bs! It's now apparent to all, including the kindergarten teacher who referred to her as "not so bright," that she is an intelligent young woman. But something that rates higher than this: she now holds her head high with confidence.

On the Grade-level Treadmill

School's like a wall, and for everybody else there's a ladder there, and they just get up on that ladder and climb over the wall. But for whatever reason, dyslexics don't know how to climb that ladder, so we've got to figure out another way to get past that wall. We've got to dig a hole under it, or find a rope to build a rope ladder, or find some other way around it. So we're constantly trying to solve a problem, and I think that's one reason why so many dyslexics become inventors and creators—because they're constantly looking for ways to beat that system, or improve that system, or change it so it makes sense to them. (Vince Flynn as quoted in Eide, 2011)

Anna's story, as well as Vince's perspective of school, can trigger all kinds of emotions. And the emotions are felt on both sides—the student/parent side and the teacher/administrator side. We are all just trying to do the best we can with the knowledge we have. This is key when it comes to how we deal with dyslexia. Lack of knowledge and lack of understanding of those with dyslexia is the biggest contributor to conflict. And the emotions follow: anger, sadness, frustration, disillusionment, and the list goes on. Placing blame is not the answer, finding the root issue and fixing it is.

Most of us have found ourselves having to take on the role of mediator between two opposing perspectives sometime in our lives. There are many instances when we can sympathize with both sides? This has happened throughout my life in both my personal life and career life. And this is the role I find myself in as I speak out on behalf of these misunderstood and often mistreated individuals with dyslexia, while experiencing the ever-encompassing demands placed on educators. I truly understand when teachers say they can't take on one more thing even if that is the worthy cause of dyslexia.

I've worked with many great teachers who have dedicated time, sweat, and tears to the students in their classrooms. Their compassion for those who struggle to learn the traditional way is evident. Unfortunately, I've also worked with some who have become burned out by all the demands and the increasing complexity of student problems. They have become hardened by the increasing lack of respect dished out by frustrated students and by the system that is spinning its wheels trying to increase student productivity. They have become disillusioned when they see that our educational system is losing sight of the individual teacher and the individual student.

Where is the student with dyslexia in all this tumultuous mix of emotions? I hate to say, but left behind and ignored. This would be understandable if we were lacking information on dyslexia. However, medical journals written in the late nineteenth century and an increasing amount of material published throughout the twentieth century tells us otherwise. The research is staggering, but it isn't reaching the key people who need it—our teachers.

When I went through my crisis as a teacher, triggered by realizing I didn't have the tools I needed to help struggling students, I stepped off the normal path and chose an unconventional route. The training I received at the Fundamental Learning Center did give me the necessary tools, but it also left me dumbfounded with the realization that the answers have been around for the past century. I wondered why I had never been exposed to even a glimpse of it throughout the pursuit of my special education degree and in the field, especially when discovering that at least 20 percent of students are somewhere on the dyslexia spectrum. The only ones who seemed to have any knowledge on the subject were those who experienced it firsthand, and that typically was the dyslexic individual or the parent of a dyslexic child. One of those parents shares her introduction into the world of dyslexia, and her story is similar to Anna's family's experience.

Phiyllis Orlowski, a public school teacher with a master's degree in reading, didn't have the tools necessary to help her own son, let alone her students who had dyslexia. It wasn't until her son Desi's struggle, despite his eagerness to learn and his obvious intelligence and creativity, that Orlowski realized she had to do something. A diagnosis would not come until the fifth grade, but the recognition of differences was confirmed in the first grade when Desi's teacher wrote on his report card: "It saddens me to see a child apparently unable to learn...I regret that I am unable to promote him to second grade." This prompted a resolve to learn more.

> This began my parental advocacy. I was a single mom with three sons to raise, but I knew I had to fight for Desi's education. I was also fighting for the life of this frustrated boy who would cling to me when it was time to go to school, crying in the morning and at night; there is no school for me! He was angry. He was sad. He wouldn't eat....By sixth grade, he was barely reading at a second grade level, and his writing skills were even lower–but I had learned a lot. (Phyllis C. Orlowski as quoted in Hubbell, 2012)

For the love of her child, Phyllis Orlowski pursued the knowledge she needed to help her son. Just as Anna's family had to fight for their rights by taking legal measures, the Orlowski family took similar measures. The process began with requesting that the district send a teacher to be trained in an Orton-Gillingham program. However, when this was denied, Ms. Orlowski made the difficult, but ultimately beneficial decision, to send Desi to a boarding school that specializes in teaching dyslexic boys. This decision ultimately cost the family a second mortgage on their house and working multiple jobs even though they received financial aid from the school and Desi's grandfather. Fortunately, it was worth the sacrifices as Desi's self-esteem increased dramatically. He learned to *really* read, reaching a sixth grade level by the end of seventh grade. Ms. Orlowski continued to pursue legal action for her own son, as well as hoping to make changes for others with dyslexia, but all the expenses and stress resulted in a dead end. "My hopes to help many dyslexic children, aside from my own, were crushed." She says of the process:

> I have learned that the due process system is grueling and flawed in many ways—it's nearly impossible to prevail. Districts succeed as single families' finances become depleted. Sadly, litigation becomes a battle between parent and school attorney. Because of confidentiality issues, key information that reveals gaps in instruction and ineffective methods rarely gets back to the teachers who might then change their practice. A family faces financial ruin while a school district simply pays an attorney through a private insurance company, burying the expenses and hiding it from the taxpayers whose own children may be the ones who struggle. (Phyllis C. Orlowski as quoted in Hubbell, 2012)

Although Ms. Orlowski's legal actions were unsuccessful, her advocacy for her son has proven fruitful as demonstrated by Desi's strong ACT scores, scoring in the top 97th percentile in the reading section.

Those who have had to fight for their child's rights know firsthand that our educational system in many ways is broken. In most cases, we should not be blaming the teacher for the neglect of our dyslexic children, because they are at the mercy of a bureaucracy much larger than themselves.

I've been asking myself and others for over ten years why there continues to be such confusion on the topic of dyslexia, and why we continue to ignore it in our schools. These questions turned up three reasons: the complexity of dyslexia, funding priorities, and the difficult process of changing established systems, in this case, our educational system. I do not claim to hold a quick fix to this complex issue, but a closer look at each may help us learn how to better advocate for those individuals who we know are suffering.

Complexity of Dyslexia

Receiving the education I needed on the subject of dyslexia did give me tools to teach dyslexic students; however, it didn't take long to discover its complexity. Dyslexic traits, both positive and negative, are as diverse as the individual. It is true that the list of common indicators found in chapter 2 can be used to help identify many with dyslexia, but some students can only be matched with one or two indicators. Is that dyslexia? I'm still not sure if my brother's struggles were due to dyslexia or just that he, like me, was slower at processing anything in print. I found that the best indication that someone truly has dyslexia was if they responded to being taught using an Orton-Gillingham-based program.

Dyslexia is on a spectrum; some are profoundly affected and some are only mildly affected. But this only describes the areas of weakness. An awareness of common strengths can be just as helpful when trying to determine if someone has dyslexia. When we see that ability doesn't seem to match up with inability, creating a sense of wonder and confusion, that can be one of the clearest indications that dyslexia is at the root of the learning issues.

It has only been in the past century that we have begun to tap into the complexity of how the brain processes, and since dyslexia is a brain-processing difference, we are still tackling its complexity. It is difficult to fully understand what it is like for these individuals. That is unless you experience it. David Boies, a dyslexic attorney who made *Time* magazine's 100 Most Influential People in the World in 2010, used an analogy that can bring better understanding.

I have one portal, I have to operate less efficiently and more slowly than I would otherwise. It doesn't affect my processing once I get information into my system, but I have an input problem. I'm a computer system with a faulty optical character recognition system. But it's not crippling because I believe that input is the least important of the functions of thinking and analysis, and there are lots of ways around it. (David Boies as quoted in Gladwell, 2013)

The diagnosis of dyslexia adds to the complexity. In most states, there are no testing tools available in schools, and families have to go outside the system to get an official diagnosis. Those who have been trained in an Orton-Gillingham program have tools for screening children and can offer an informal diagnosis; however, a formal diagnosis can only be obtained through a licensed psychologist, psychiatrist, or physician. And only a few of these individuals have the specialized training necessary for making a diagnosis. In many schools, even the mention of the word *dyslexia* creates controversy and confusion, as alluded to by an interaction between a teacher and a parent who was asking for help for her son. "We don't recognize the D-word. It would be so much easier if your son had ADHD, there's medicine for that."

Despite its complexity, the answer is not to ignore it and hope students can learn to get around it. All students can benefit from the strategies that the dyslexic child needs. And all students benefit from early intervention when they are not learning through the traditional methods. Continuing down the same path when it isn't working is like watching a child who is drowning and encouraging them to simply swim to the edge. Offering them empty encouragement and prodding while watching them flounder in frustration will not make them learn to swim. The same is true with the child floundering in the classroom—they need someone to come alongside them, teaching in ways that bring connections to the confusion of print.

Funding Priorities: Change is Expensive (or is it?)

"It costs about $23,000 a year to keep a person in prison. It costs about $11,000 a year to educate a child, so if you care about the economics of this, that's a no-brainer" (Margie Gillis as quoted in Hubbell, 2012)

School districts have had to learn to operate with decreasing funds over the past decade, creating a hot-button debate for many. Everyone seems to have a different idea when it comes to prioritizing the limited funds. Increasing standardization has led districts to purchase updated curriculum, assessment tools, and new programs that claim to increase student productivity.

Unfortunately, the emphasis has gone away from the individual student and toward meeting national, state, and district mandates. Flowery descriptions of the latest new thing with little to no recognition of differing learning styles, sell products. Publishing companies have talented sales personnel who can make their curriculum and programs sound like it can produce miracles, with little to no substantive research to back them up. A lot of money can be spent on the latest, greatest materials, only resulting in the ever-increasing trial and error attempts to increase student productivity and test scores.

Although I understand the desperation school administrators are feeling with increasing pressure to bring test scores up, that does not excuse the discriminatory treatment some of our students are experiencing. Most disabilities are addressed through the special education process, but dyslexia is too often ignored. Yes, they are given some help through the existing programs, but too often the help does not match what research tells us works for those with dyslexia.

In my experience, schools would rather invest in expensive curriculum and programs than the investment of giving teachers specialized training and materials for students who require alternative teaching methods. Teachers of students who qualify for special education services must demonstrate that students are progressing; however, the word *progress* is used very loosely. Catching up to their peers is not an expectation. This attitude is voiced in an actual conversation between a teacher and a parent: "We don't have the money to provide the best education…We just have to show the student is making progress."

Difficult Process of Changing Established Traditional Systems

"For nonconformity the world whips you with its displeasure. And dyslexia is nothing if not nonconformity, the very essence of being different and apart." (Gladwell, 2013)

Much publicity on the national crisis in education has surfaced over the last decade. The big push behind the need for transformation in our educational system was made more public with the No Child Left Behind initiative and the publication of how individual schools were performing. The pressure to compete globally has become a driving force in our schools.

The increase in student-to-teacher ratio and the push to teach complex subject matter earlier in the child's school career have made allowing for individual pacing almost nonexistent. Many struggling students have been left in the dust, even those who receive services in special education or academic intervention groups. Nationwide, 32% of fourth graders were reading below Basic level in 2013, according to the National Center for Education Statistics (NCES). This is just one report. Margie Gillis, the president of Literacy How, is a teacher and researcher whose goal is to teach teachers to implement research-based practices in the classroom. She offers additional perspective by breaking down the statistics according to race.

> Are you aware of the percentages of kids who are not reading on grade level in fourth grade? Do you know that 88 percent of our African-American students are reading below grade level? Eighty-five percent of our Hispanic students? Fifty-nine percent of our Caucasian students? This isn't just kids who live in poverty, this is across the board. This is all kids struggling. For what? Why? Because we are not doing what works, and we know what works. We have thirty years of research coming out of places like Haskins Laboratories. People have dedicated their research lives to exploring the most effective ways for teaching reading. Why isn't it happening? How can you sleep at night knowing this? (Margie Gillis as quoted in Hubbell, 2012)

These statistics include all children, and tells me that our nation's illiteracy rate will not improve unless we address each student's learning needs. Where have we gone wrong? And what will it take to turn things around? Marcia Henry, a past president of the International Dyslexia Association gives us an overview of the history of education, which can help us see where we went wrong and where we are currently headed. (Hubbell, 2012)

When public education was mandated in the mid- to late- 1800s, children were taught using phonetically based primers, often with a moral message. However, this all changed in the 1930s when a group of professors thought that method was too slow. They advised that children should memorize words. The whole word, or look-say method, became the method of teaching reading. In *Dick and Jane*, children were taught that the word *Jane* represented the little girl, not that Jane started with the / j / sound.

The whole word or look-say method evolved into the whole-language approach in the 1980s and 1990s. Good literature became the emphasis with teachers guiding students to figure out words using context, visual cues, and story structure. Again, the teaching of phonics was not a part of this approach.

Ever since 2003 when the National Reading Panel turned our emphasis towards research-based reading instruction instead of the next feel-good approach, most schools started to strive to implement the five components of reading instruction. Our public schools are waffling, however, with a tug-of-war over differing philosophies. It was only two years ago when the school district where I was teaching, hired—at great expense, I might add—a reading consultant who embraced and pushed the whole-language approach.

When public schools taught using the look-say method, it worked for children with good visual memory, but not for our dyslexic students and many others who need language to be taught using the components and approaches discussed in chapter 3. Both the look-say method and the whole-language approach do not teach the phonetic system, a huge stumbling block for many of our children.

So what will it take to turn things around? I want to believe that school districts will demand research-based instruction. My fear is that we will continue to lump dyslexia in the general category of a learning disability and disregard the distinct characteristics and the need for specialized remediation and accommodations. I fear that we will continue down the same road of denial and ignorance when it comes to the D-word—*Dyslexia.* My hope lies in the message reaching those who may have some influence over future decisions to provide appropriate teacher training and curriculum for *all students*, not just those who have good visual memory.

Many who don't work in the school system wonder what a typical classroom looks like after the teeter-totter effect of mandated changes. What does it look like from both teacher and student perspective? The stresses of a teacher are great as they have to keep up with the day-to-day demands in the classroom while learning the next "best" thing, only to find that next year there will be a "new and improved" thing to learn and implement. The result: when teacher is stressed, student is stressed, especially when they aren't learning through traditional methods.

Individuality has been removed from the classroom as both teacher and student are expected to conform to and embrace the next great thing. In *The Ripple Effect*, author and educational consultant Davis Laughlin touches on the history and trends in education.

> Throughout the history of public education in America, one of the main goals has been to produce compliant, robotic learners who will be able to move out into the workforce and become compliant, robotic employees. The relationship between teacher and student is often business-like and missing any human warmth....In this age of pacing guides and curriculum maps, teachable moments are fading away into the cold world of impersonal, mechanical classrooms. Albert Einstein said it best.

"It is a miracle that curiosity survives formal education." (Laughlin, 2015)

"Lazy" or "unmotivated" labels are often the rationalization behind students not learning. Labeling is much easier than trying to find out how to teach them. Even when we want to teach using more engaging methods or teach to a particular student's learning style needs, it is discouraged because it may slow down the rest of the class. Teaching and learning has become how to perform, not create!

How do students respond? That will be discussed at greater length in chapter 6, but one student's perspective speaks for many when it comes to their view of today's education process. These are the words of a thirteen-year-old student of Davis Laughlin's.

> On a scale of 1–10, the amount of any real thinking required at school is a two. I hardly ever have to think. I can do school without it. I have become more of a robot. I have been trained well. As far as questioning why we study the things we study, I quit doing that a long time ago. It doesn't do any good. Asking that question just makes the teachers mad. I just do what I'm told; I hardly ever see any real purpose or meaning in any of it.

While this paints a discouraging picture, there are some areas, we have made great strides in; one particular area is in the field of autism. When I see the lengths we've gone to assure that our public schools have the knowledge necessary to help teachers work with their students on the autism spectrum, it gives me hope that we can move forward for those with dyslexia.

Autism versus Dyslexia

Walking down the hall the first week of school, I saw Calvin looking as though he were hugging the wall. His back was to me and others as he slithered down the hall, shutting us and anyone who might venture by out of his world. Another day, in the hall just outside his second grade classroom, Calvin was sprawled on his belly across the floor causing those walking by to have to gingerly step around and over him in order to get to their destination.

Calvin is a high-functioning autistic boy with whom I worked from his second through sixth grades. While his amazing intellectual abilities intrigued me, his social awkwardness baffled me. Those with autism vary in how they deal with the social complexities of our world as much as their individual personalities vary. When I began my career in special education, I knew very little about autism. Over the years, after many opportunities to attend professional development on autism and receiving support from consultants, I received numerous resources and tips. All of this helped me not only become a better teacher but also gain some understanding into the thinking and complexities of these unique individuals.

Calvin had a difficult beginning to his school career, but with much support both in school and at home, he made remarkable progress. By the time he moved up to middle school, he was accepted by his peers, and they genuinely appreciated his strengths academically and especially his ability to retain trivial facts. In Calvin's case, many of his classmates were with him throughout his elementary years, which helped with their acceptance of his strengths as well as his social awkwardness.

I share his story to show the contrast between how we work with those on the autism spectrum as compared to the dyslexic student. Throughout my years in teaching, more than half of professional development opportunities were on autism. Many districts hire autism consultants to assist general education and special education staff. Depending on the individual student, extra staff are hired to give those with more severe needs individualized help. Extra materials and resources are bought to help each child to reach their fullest potential academically and socially.

In contrast, dyslexia continues to be ignored in our schools. When considering the prevalence of both, it is even more baffling. According to the Centers for Disease Control and Prevention (2014), one in sixty-eight children are on the autism spectrum. The common estimation for the prevalence of dyslexia is one in five children. When considering the difference, why have we leapt with great effort onto the autism bandwagon while disregarding those who struggle due to dyslexia?

While I don't know the answer to this question, I see it as a challenge for those of us who can influence change. All students with dyslexia should be entitled to an appropriate education, not just those who can afford special schools or private tutoring.

Currently, our educational system seems to be blind to the fact that those with dyslexia are denied appropriate remediation and accommodations. The system does not yet have a vision for how addressing this issue can help us meet the increasing demands to bring about student improvement, let alone change the futures of millions of children. Whether this blindness is due to the complexity of dyslexia, funding issues, or the fact that changing established system can be a daunting task, is irrelevant. The bottom line: will we do something about it?

Myth: Dyslexia is a vision problem.
Busted:

> A new brain imaging study appears to rule out one potential cause of dyslexia, finding that vision problems don't lead to the common reading disorder....It has importance from a practical viewpoint. It means you shouldn't focus on the visual system as a way to diagnose dyslexia or treat dyslexia. (Guinevere Eden as quoted in Hubbell, 2012)

6

? Some Children are just Unmotivated ?
Labeling by Self and Others

Dalton's Story: Just the Right Person for the Job

Long, lanky legs carried Dalton through the middle school doors, grinning with a rare, mischievous grin that said, *Let's have some fun today!* This was not typical for Dalton, but over the years, his classmates had come to recognize that there were two very different personalities inside him. This was the Dalton who would bring them an extraordinary day—a welcome out-of-the-norm day.

The bell rang, and students were expected to be sitting in class, ready to listen, take notes, and participate in the daily routines—an expectation far out of reach for Dalton.

Sitting was particularly difficult for him as he bounced around like a ball in a pinball machine, engaging in banter that only middle schoolers fully understand. The words *sit down* were met with a look of *Ha-ha! If only that could happen!* But in this state of mind, Dalton didn't even care if his actions brought a reprimand; he was living in the moment, and his actions stemmed from an internal wiring similar to someone who just drank 32 ounces of Red Bull.

This was Dalton off his meds for ADHD, which only happened on the rare occasion when he pretended to take his pill before leaving home. This would have happened more frequently if he had thought he could get away with it. After all, Dalton off of meds could bring smiles, laughter, and the transformation of an otherwise normal humdrum day. Unfortunately, our schools are not designed to adapt to this type of free-spirited energy; students have to adapt to our traditional classroom setting. Ideally, we would try to guide this energy to a creative flow that would lead to learning. But in reality, with many like Dalton, ADHD affects the ability to focus to such an extent that they can't complete normal day-to-day tasks.

The only thing more powerful than Dalton's energetic, jovial personality is the pill he takes for his ADHD, which he had been taking ever since kindergarten. This particular day was not typical for Dalton. His normal demeanor at school, when he actually swallowed his pill, was shy and reserved with a look of wanting to blend into the woodwork. What compounded his quiet demeanor were the excruciating frustrations he experienced at being unable to perform the everyday tasks that required reading and writing and even math.

What was at the root of those disabilities? At an earlier point in my teaching career, I would have chalked it up to ADHD and lack of motivation as the main factors. But after working with dyslexic students for some time, I realized that Dalton's academic struggles most likely stemmed from an undiagnosed dyslexia, probably at the profound end of the spectrum.

I met Dalton when he was beginning the seventh grade, and only had the privilege of working with him two years. It didn't take long to discover he was unable to read or write yet, which initially made me question his overall intellectual capacity. With time, however, I realized he demonstrated an ability to comprehend and figure out answers to complex questions, and sometimes his insight exceeded his peers. When information was presented to him by auditory means, without distractions of having to process visual material, he often could take and pass tests. He also made good improvements with a multisensory teaching program, using Orton-Gillingham methods. Progress took him from being a nonreader, who couldn't spell enough to write, to reading and writing at the second grade level. This confirmed my suspicions of dyslexia since success with an Orton-Gillingham program is the best indicator. Given that Dalton was on the profound end of the dyslexia spectrum in my assessment, I'm sure if he had continued with the same type of remediation, he could have come closer to reaching his full potential.

Throughout Dalton's elementary years, numerous strategies and programs were tried, but each were met with an ever-increasing frustration. By the time I met him in middle school, his happy, full-of-life grin was only evident when he was off his meds or when he was done with school. It was replaced with an almost constant look of defeat.

As educators, we're trained to treat each student equally and fairly. But it's impossible to remove the emotional factor of teaching. Some students tug on our heartstrings more than others. Dalton was one of those students for me. The stigma of not being able to read or write had greatly marred his self-perception. When working with children who qualify for special education services, their Individual Education Plan, or IEP, drives the direction we take. We strive to help them meet goals that indicate at least some progress, and we implement the specified accommodations to help them participate with peers as much as possible. Unfortunately, the emphasis is on students' weaknesses with strengths being downplayed or ignored. Working on goals that emphasize weaknesses becomes another daily reminder that they don't measure up to their peers, and that reminder gradually erodes their self-esteem.

Students need other opportunities that can help them discover strengths. Art, music, and athletics are so important to the overall educational experience. Fortunately, in middle school, Dalton discovered he had a strong athletic ability, and he especially excelled at track, cross-country, and wrestling. Finally, he could have something to be proud of, and something others would look up to him for. This affirmation brought a greater drive to push himself, and his perseverance and stamina caused his classmates to take notice.

In addition to athletic ability, he has the ability to see what needs to be done without being told, at least when working with his hands. Dalton's strong work ethic is a trait that makes others want to work alongside him. This was especially evident when participating in mission projects at his church. Aren't these qualities that all employers are looking for when hiring?

While in school, Dalton sees himself as different and flawed. The effects were written on his face, in his body language, and even in how he conversed. His whole demeanor changes when he is doing what he is good at. He talks more, he laughs more, he smiles more! He is yet another example of why we must stop ignoring and denying dyslexia in our schools. The damage for many is irreversible.

Fortunately for Dalton, he has a strong family support system and a natural drive that I'm sure will be his ticket to success in future endeavors. His ability to just see what needs to be done, with an enthusiasm that is contagious, makes you want to be on his team—to be on his team in sports, work, and play. If only this enthusiasm could be tapped into when in the classroom.

Self-perception and Its Impact

What does it feel like—how does it feel, to be chronically, day after day, week after week, month after month, and for a great many children, year after year—not good enough? Not good enough at something that they know is important, that they know is causing them to fall behind, that they can't seem to get good enough at achieving, and that they can't hide because their family, friends, and peers know about it too? What is the effect of chronically feeling "not good enough" about your learning? (David Boulton)

Colin Poole, a successful artist and sculptor, gives us an analogy of how he experienced the chronic feeling of not being good enough. He says, "It was like crawling over broken glass on your hands and knees. It was uncomfortable from start to finish." Grade school was the most challenging, but in high school and college, Poole says he figured out some "coping mechanisms for figuring it out and how to work around things (he) couldn't do." (Hubbell, 2012)

But how do those early experiences influence who we become? That varies with each individual: some using their struggles and strengths to find great success, and some never really recovering, making one poor life choice after another. One has to wonder why illiteracy in our prisons is at such an alarming rate—85% of all juveniles who come into contact with the juvenile court system are functionally illiterate. (www.invisiblechildren.org/2010/11/18/75-of-inmates-are-illiterate-19-are-completely-illiterate-ruben-rosario/)

The old saying *You are What You Hear* is more truth than not, but it extends far beyond the sense of hearing. In the classroom, a student becomes what they see and experience as differences—differences in how we look, differences in the ability to make friends, and even differences in how we learn. Comparing ourselves to others is a human characteristic that begins early in life and never really ends. In the classroom, it is impossible to level the playing field to the point of making everyone feel good about themselves because children instinctively pick up even subtle differences.

Teachers often don't know the anguish some children are going through. Many hold in their frustrations and wait until they get home to express it. If students don't communicate how they're really feeling, the focus naturally goes to those students who demand our attention, and there are plenty of them.

Typically, students come to kindergarten with a thirst for learning and a desire to be accepted and liked. They come to school like a beautifully transformed butterfly, slurping up the nectar of knowledge as they fly from flower to flower, excited and ready to soak up all that we have to offer, and continued success leads to positive school experiences. However, what about those children who continually experience failure or those who struggle to make friends? What happens to them?

> Samuel T. Orton, M.D. was one of the first researchers to describe the emotional aspects of dyslexia. According to his research, the majority of dyslexic preschoolers are happy and well adjusted. Their emotional problems begin to develop when early reading instruction does not match their learning style. Over the years, the frustration mounts as classmates surpass the dyslexic student in reading skills. (The International Dyslexia Association)

The early years of school can make or break a child. Their experiences during these crucial years play a huge part in developing a positive or negative self-image, which in turn affects how they respond to those around them. If a child is guided into discovering their strengths with an optimistic outlook on any weakness, they are much more likely to remain happy and content. Children come into this world wanting to learn and succeed, and most want to please others. This is true for the early years, and only tends to change if they are confronted with continual failure, despite the fact that they are trying very hard.

Children who face the daily reality that they can't do what their classmates can do, with their weaknesses as the main emphasis, tend to blame themselves. Children who are caught in this cycle of chronically feeling "not good enough" about their learning need courage and perseverance just to face each day. Parents are usually the ones who have to pick up the pieces when their child comes home from school in tears, and when they beg each morning not to make them go. For most of these children, the initial begging eventually turns to a reluctant acceptance although the scars remain.

Each year becomes a new learning adjustment as students have to figure out expectations of each new teacher and how to survive. Glenn Bailey, a multimillionaire entrepreneur who dropped out of school because "it wasn't adding much to the strengths he intended to use in the real world," shares his personal experience of what it feels like to try desperately to fit in.

I was also very curious, and strangely enough that became an issue at school. I'd ask questions like, 'Why's this?' or 'Why's that?' and that was treated like a problem. Teaching was regarded as a one-way street, but I really learned best through inter-action. My biggest problem was in English. Being able to read is the 'face of intelligence' you present to society, and if you can't read, people just auto-matically assume that you're stupid. What happens to individuals with dyslexia in school is that read-ing becomes this big fifty-pound weight that just drags your whole body under. So I didn't have much confidence in any department of academics. I just thought I wasn't that bright. I called myself 'the Shadow' because I was just trying to get by day by day. (Glenn Bailey as quoted in Eide, 2011)

The self-blame that children with dyslexia experience often leads to feelings of isolation. Many feel like they are the only one going through a rough time. Their embarrass-ment and shame can result in spending their lunchtime in the bathroom or off in a secluded corner during recess, both of which I have witnessed. Philip Schultz shares the emotional impact of not knowing why he couldn't learn like others. "My ignorance of my dyslexia only intensified my sense of isolation and hopelessness. Ignorance is perhaps the most painful aspect of a learning disability" (Schultz, 2011)

Throughout my years in teaching, a common discussion revolved around the emotional baggage that children bring from home, and the affect it has on their performance in the classroom. However, what about the flipside—the emotional baggage they carry from school to home.

It's time we look at what children are bringing home from their daily struggles in the classroom. The perspectives of both the dyslexic individual and experts in the field can offer insight into two important questions: What is the emotional baggage dyslexics carry around? And how do dyslexics respond to the emotional baggage?

What is the Emotional Baggage Dyslexics Carry Around?

> I never meant to be annoying, forgetful, delayed, overwhelmed, and dumb-sounding and—looking. I never wanted to be made fun of or anger my teachers or keep an entire class late because I didn't understand a concept. But that's what often happened as a consequence of my learning disability. (Schultz, 2011)

Our society tends to deal with dyslexia in one of three ways. Some try to build self-esteem, some tear down with labels, and many just ignore it. Of course, if we have to choose, building self-esteem is the better choice, but children can be very insightful when it comes to distinguishing between truth and empty words. Children must have some form of success in order to have self-esteem, and they are experts at intuitively recognizing when praise is earned or rooted in truth versus empty feel-good words. To truly instill self-esteem, we must guide them into discovering what they are good at.

Some don't see building a child's self-esteem as productive, especially when the child is not keeping up with their classmates. Their response is to dish out labels, verbally and nonverbally. Of course this stems from the undercurrent of desperation and pressure to keep all students learning at the same rate. As discussed previously, people often respond to things they don't understand from a black & white perspective. When it comes to things we don't understand, we tend to paint with a broad brush. Here's just a few of the more common things said of those who have dyslexia and other learning disabilities and how they are treated.

Lazy

The teachers said I was lazy. (Bruce Jenner)

I went to school in the 1950s, and in my experience, no one recognized a condition called dyslexia. I am very verbal, so people could listen to my thinking when I was talking and realize, 'This guy's got a good head on his shoulders.' So what I got all the time was, "You're not applying yourself. If you would just apply yourself, you would do so much better.'" (Stephen J. Cannell, Writer, Producer as quoted in Hubbell, 2012)

The teacher consistently reports "laziness" and "willfulness" which I see as a cry for help. (Parent)

The reading teacher improperly stated, "You don't have dyslexia. You're just lazy." (Parent)

Underperformance

Often individuals who decode relatively well but still read slowly aren't identified as dyslexic. Instead they get noticed for underperformance, inattention, lack of persistence with reading, or their tendency to avoid reading altogether. (Eide, 2011)

Parents and teachers see a bright, enthusiastic child who is not learning to read and write. Time and again, dyslexics and their parents hear, "He's such a bright child; if only he would try harder." Ironically, no one knows exactly how hard the dyslexic is trying. (The International Dyslexia Association)

Retarded, Stupid

I have a dear friend who's a neurologist and incredibly dyslexic and was told he was retarded as a kid. He eventually went on to be the head of pediatric neurosurgery at Children's Hospital in San Diego. (Sarah Joy Brown as quoted in Hubbell, 2012)

I just didn't feel confident enough to read in front of other kids because, even in special education, all they do is look at you and laugh. "You're stupid! You're retarded!" What I would do is act tough. "I ain't doing that. Send me to the principal, but I ain't doing it." (Billy Blanks, Inventor of Tae Bo exercise program as quoted in Hubbell, 2012)

She's an Academy Award-winning actress, comedian, radio host, and television personality. In addition to her success on stage and screen, Whoopi has written three books, two of which are for children.

It's hard to imagine that this successful woman once struggled in school, hearing words such as "dumb" and "stupid" directed at her. (http://dyslexia.yale. edu/goldberg.html; The Yale Center for Dyslexia & Creativity)

Troublemaker

No matter how much my teachers tried to drag me through math to some sort of understanding, I just didn't get it. And because I carried a calculator in high school, I was considered a troublemaker. (Hubbell, 2012)

Humiliation

Once at school, I had to sit on a chair in the hall the entire day because I couldn't do my work. I told the teachers that I didn't understand it, but they thought that I just wasn't trying. (Desi Gialanella as quoted in Hubbell, 2012)

Humiliation really affects your life when you're a kid. You accept that you're no good at this. (Billy Bob Thornton as quoted in Hubbell, 2012)

The teacher held up a paper and asked, "Whose is this?" From our seats, we could all see how sloppy it was. Mine. The teacher went on and on about unacceptable work. Then he told me to leave, out loud, in front of the entire class. (Hubbell, 2012)

When I was in school, the teachers would send me to detention. One time they had me in the detention room for thirty days with no books, no nothing, just me in the room. And then they pulled me out of the room to take some test. I did very poorly on that test because your mind kind of slows down when you are closed up like that. (Zach Capriotti, Inmate at State Correctional Institute as quoted in Hubbell, 2012)

How Do Dyslexics Respond to Their Emotional Baggage?

Shame, anxiety, fear, anger, and frustration are emotions we all share at one time or another. But imagine feeling some of these emotions every day, or at least every school day. Our emotions trigger responses, sometimes inwardly and sometimes outwardly. Each of us, with our unique personalities, make daily choices that shape who we become. Children react to how others perceive them, and responses are unique, depending on the child's personality and the level of humiliation they endure. For those with dyslexia, here are some common responses to the menagerie of emotions they experience.

Class Clown

And when not much makes sense, you only have a couple of places to go. You could be the class clown. What are you going to do when you can't tie your shoes in the fourth grade because you don't know your left hand from your right hand? You know everyone's laughing at you because you're a joke. You may have a secret feeling that you're really not an idiot, but there are so many things that other kids can do just fine, and you can't do at all. The only refuge is to act like you're making them laugh on purpose. Maybe that's why Jay Leno became Jay Leno. (Hubbell, 2012)

(Comedian Jim Carrey shares his difficulties with dyslexia, including how one teacher, Lucy Dervaitis, encouraged his sense of humor)

Obviously, he wanted attention. So rather than discipline him for disrupting the class, she asked him to put together an act and perform it for the class at the end of the school day, on the condition that he would do his work and not disturb the class. He thought this was a great idea and went along with it. Jim would impersonate popular figures like actor John Wayne or Elvis. He'd jump around and contort his face. The students loved it, asking for a Jim show when they got bored. Lucy, however, would usually say that they had to wait for the end of the day or a special occasion. Jim bonded with Lucy Dervaitis from the first day of class. It's no wonder. She believed in him. It was a breakthrough for Jim, whom you might have already guessed is Jim Carrey, hugely successful stand-up comedian and star of many successful films such as *Dumb and Dumber*, *Mask*, *Liar Liar* and *The Truman Show*. (Dyslexia HELP: http://dyslexiahelp.umich.edu)

In the classroom environment, a lot of the ways that children who are dyslexic will mask their inability to read is to draw attention to themselves. That sounds strange, but that's what they'll do. They will make jokes and carry on until the class is riled up and the teacher is off task, and then they won't have to read out loud....The class clown finds another way to get attention, since he can't get any attention for doing good work. The trauma that children go through is just amazing. (Robin Winternitz as quoted in Hubbell, 2012)

Disrupting Class/Lack of Cooperation/Resistance

Eventually the students find themselves in a situation with expectations that they can't possibly meet. So they either continue to be sweet and charming, or find other ways to occupy themselves by disrupting the class or tuning out. All of this is typical, and the usual response is to blame a child's speech problem, or blame a lack of maturity, or blame this, that, and the other. (Diana Hanbury King as quoted in Hubbell, 2012)

Anger/Hostility

And there is the aggressive one, who is always acting out. These children are just so angry. They know they are as smart as the other kids, but they also know they can't do the same things, and they have no idea why....I've seen successful adults, extremely confident people who run businesses, break down and start crying when the subject turns to writing on the blackboard in third grade. Those are serious wounds, and I think we need to do everything we can to stop inflicting them. (Robin Winternitz as quoted in Hubbell, 2012)

The shame of disappointing adults and disappointing oneself then turns to resentment of those who seem to hold unachievable expectations. This psychological trap–for which there seems no reasonable way out–leads alternately to anger at others and anger at oneself. Anger at oneself, in turn, can quickly be transformed into a chronic sense of helplessness and even depression. (Moats & Dakin, 2008)

Giving Up/Dropping Out

When you can't do something everybody else in the room can do, you give yourself the label of 'dumb.' And the kids who have labeled themselves 'dumb' are kids who are fearful of every new situation at school. There are fewer students with learning difficulties in their junior and senior years. They aren't there anymore. They have chosen to leave school. (Joan Soner as quoted in Hubbell, 2012)

20% of the average freshman class will drop out of high school. (Is it a coincidence that 20% of our

population has dyslexia?) (Children's Defense Fund:
Children in Kansas)

The real shame is that the victims of bullying, certainly dyslexic ones, don't understand that the way
their mind processes information isn't a matter of
weakness or blame; that their inability to answer
back isn't their fault. The dyslexic's mind is a muscle
that remembers to protect itself against its memory
of painful events. It **shuts down** when it becomes
overloaded in order to spare itself further stress; this
happens instantaneously, without warning. (Schultz,
2011)

Bad Behavior

Research has shown that the high percentage of
young offenders in prisons are found to have dyslexia....They don't know how to deal with their
dyslexia, get stressed, cause problems in school, start
doing crime, and everything in their futures goes
wrong....With dyslexia, time (spent) in education
will be a time of hell and confusion. It is not the
dyslexia that causes the problems; not understanding is the problem. (Milner, 2012)

Eighty-five percent of the prison population reads below a sixth grade level. (Hubbell, 2012)

When dyslexia is not found and treated early on, it tends to snowball. As kids get more and more behind in school, they may become more and more frustrated, feeling like a failure. Often, self-esteem problems lead to bad behavior and other problems. (Fundamental Learning Center)

Anxiety/Stress

"I was a functional illiterate," says Tom Cruise, who hid his problem for years…."When I was about 7 years old, I had been labeled dyslexic. I'd try to concentrate on what I was reading, then I'd get to the end of the page and have very little memory of anything I'd read. I would go blank, feel anxious, nervous, bored, frustrated, dumb. I would get angry. My legs would actually hurt when I was studying. My head ached. All through school and well into my career, I felt like I had a secret." (People.com, July 21, 2003, vol. 60, no. 3)

Anxiety causes human beings to avoid whatever frightens them. The dyslexic is no exception. However, many teachers and parents misinterpret this avoidance behavior as laziness. (The International Dyslexia Association)

We know that chronic stress affects brain processing and brain ability, and I can't think of any group of people that goes through more stress than children with dyslexia, spending day after day in a classroom environment that is not designed for them. Even if a talent may be there, it's often disguised. (Gordon Sherman as quoted in Hubbell, 2012)

Self Name-calling

My first grade son is having trouble w/reading and writing mainly.....He reads very slow and just guesses at words he sounds out....I HATE seeing him shut down on me and calling himself a loser or stupid. (Parent)

Researchers have learned that when typical learners succeed, they credit their own efforts for their success. When they fail, they tell themselves to try harder. However, when the dyslexic succeeds, he is likely to attribute his success to luck. When he fails, he simply sees himself as stupid. (The International Dyslexia Association)

I was never told by students, or certainly not by my parents, that I was stupid. Nobody ever said that to me. I said that to me. I put that label on myself. (Stephen J. Cannell as quoted in Hubbell, 2012)

In Summary

How the dyslexic individual responds to the daily reminder of their differences is what ultimately determines who they become. Will they become hardened, angry, and resentful, which often leads to life choices that could be devastating? Or will they face it head-on and fight through the struggles to become success stories similar to those in this book. It is mostly determined by the individual going through it, but those around him can influence and steer him in a productive manner.

The day-to-day choices we make in our interactions with others can greatly affect the lives of those around us. Will we build up with our words or tear down? Will we take the time to learn the facts or will we continue to ignore? Will we strive to understand or remain ignorant? These questions are especially pertinent to how we deal with dyslexia. The answers to these questions can be life-altering. Our response can bring hope and encouragement, or defeat and devastation!

> For every remote miss who becomes stronger, there are countless near misses who are crushed by what they have been through. (Gladwell, 2013)

Myth: Children with dyslexia are unmotivated.
Busted:

> Dyslexia is not caused by lack of motivation or interest in reading. Lack of motivation to read and write may be a consequence of dyslexia because reading is very taxing and difficult for a dyslexic individual. (Moats & Dakin, 2008)

> Any child, and particularly one who is dyslexic, needs some recognition of how hard he is working as well as tangible evidence that all his effort makes a difference; this can come in the form of improvement on a graph of his fluency rates or receiving a grade on the content of his written work rather than its form. (Shaywitz, 2003)

7

? Reversals = Dyslexia ?
Reversing the Negatives into Positives

Nicole's Story: Finding Treasure in the Turmoil

"Why do you hang out with them?" This simple question was a turning point in Nicole's thriving social life. The two girls watched them as they whispered and giggled just loud enough for the new girl in school to hear. "Look what she's wearing! She must have just crawled out of a dumpster!" The new girl's timid smile turned downcast as she continued through the cafeteria line. Her slumped shoulders made it evident that she heard the mean girls' comment.

This kind of cattiness was becoming an everyday occurrence as the popular group was slowly evolving into the "mean girls club." Nicole used to be proud that she was accepted by the elite popular group. However, she began to question herself and the group she belonged to as she witnessed an ever-increasing bully mentality. Those who were not considered part of the popular group started questioning Nicole's judgment, saying, "You're too nice to be hanging around with them!"

Nicole realized she had to make a move. She had to take a stand even though it would mean she would no longer be part of the envied popular crowd. The notion of the "popular" group continues to be alive and well in today's schools, and with this strong cultural reality, how could someone possibly put the "mean girls" in their place. Nicole mustered up the courage to confront them, saying she didn't want to have anything to do with them if they continued their rudeness. You can imagine how quickly the word spread—about as fast as if someone were to yell, "GIRL FIGHT!" While most of the mean girls snubbed Nicole after that, one friend did hear her message. In the end, the confrontation earned Nicole the respect of many in her school, and eventually, the dissolving of the mean girls club.

Given Nicole's own life challenges, it seems unlikely that she would become such a strong and courageous champion for others. But from her first breath, it was clear to her parents and medical professionals that Nicole was a fighter. She was born with a heart defect that required surgeries at the ages of two months, ten months, and two years. At the age of nine, she was also diagnosed with dyslexia, another layer of pain added to the deep pool of physical and emotional trauma she had already endured.

Nevertheless, she refused to pity herself or accept pity from others. She responded to the challenges by showing deep compassion for others and honing in her natural leadership abilities, two qualities that were evident when she singlehandedly dissolved the mean girls club.

Nicole started using these strengths long before the confrontation with the mean girls at the middle school she attended. In fact, they were evident at a very young age, before she even knew that her struggles in the classroom stemmed from dyslexia. She came up with the idea to create a lemonade stand to make money for the American Heart Association and the Ronald McDonald House, both having had a personal impact in her young life. What began as a simple idea grew into a project that eventually earned over $8,600.

Nicole has grown a heart of gold in place of her once defective heart. Partner this with a fighting, never-give-up personality, and she can conquer whatever she puts her mind to. Even when facing the struggle to learn by traditional methods, she possessed a determination that defied all odds. Her mother, a first grade teacher at the school she attended, wondered what was causing Nicole's difficulties. She wasn't making the stereotypical letter reversals, so her mother thought, *It can't be dyslexia, she isn't reversing her letters.* Equating dyslexia with reversing letters and numbers continues to be a common misconception. Concern for her daughter eventually led to pursuing testing outside the school district, and Nicole was given a formal diagnosis of dyslexia. Soon after, she qualified for special education services.

My work with Nicole was just beginning when I observed her unquenchable drive and desire to learn. Even with her dyslexia, which made daily school activities difficult, she pushed herself to do what was hard. Particularly uncomfortable for her is reading out loud and giving presentations and speeches. And yet, she voluntarily participates in several groups that require these skills. Her desire to bring about positive change motivates her to step out of her comfort zone.

Others took notice of Nicole's drive and passion, and she was offered many leadership opportunities. She was chosen as the class representative for Reno County Youth Leadership. In that role, she spearheaded fundraisers for both the animal shelter and the Boys & Girls Club. Teachers chose her to go on a weekend Kiwanis Key Leader Leadership Camp, which teaches leadership skills. She is involved in the Hutchinson Community Foundation in which she shadows community leaders. She watches how they make positive additions to the community, such as adding bike trails, downtown renovations, and bringing healthy restaurants into the area. Her school counselor also noticed her compassion and her ability to stand up for what's right, which made Nicole an obvious choice for Communities That Care, an organization that works to produce community change for reducing youth violence, alcohol and tobacco use, and delinquency.

Nicole is well on her way to reaching her full potential, and while she is already contributing to her community, she still has to maneuver through the remaining two years of high school and college. Because of her dyslexia, school still has its challenges, so she shared her insight into how teachers can be more helpful. Nicole appreciates teachers who maintain control of the classroom; unnecessary drama and clowning around just create distractions that add to the struggle. She thinks that teachers who "give easy A's aren't helping students at all." She adds, "How will that help me the next year? Just teach me. I'm not looking for the 'fun teacher' like everyone else, just the one who can teach." Nicole added that she needs instruction to be organized, with complex concepts taught in a step-by-step manner, and learns better with the patient rather than the high pressure approach.

Teaching strategies are important, but Nicole says that respect is also a key aspect that motivates her to want to learn. She respects teachers who give students a chance rather than reacting to a label, whether it is a student who has a bad reputation or a student who learns differently. Respect that is given is returned, with compassion always at the forefront of her thinking.

Nicole's big heart is part of what makes her unique and self-confident. She refuses to allow dyslexia to keep her from meeting goals, making her a perfect example of how strengths outweigh weaknesses. Her visionary and leadership skills, as well as her compassion for others, were evident at a young age when she decided to open a lemonade stand. She has been exercising these gifts ever since. Transforming the mean girls club, participation in organizations that can transform her community, and being a role model student, with the guts to speak her mind, are just a few ways she is already using her strengths.

Nicole is a source of inspiration, spunk, and giftedness who is already bringing hope and encouragement to others. Since she is already doing great things, just think what is to come!

Strengths Outweigh Weaknesses

My son is special not despite, but because of, his dyslexia. He is learning he is good and capable the way an archaeologist learns the history of the earth, inch by deliberate and all-consuming inch: the way we all learn to love what is weakest and most confounding about ourselves, because and despite and in deference to what is essential about us. (Schultz, 2011)

Sometimes I am asked why I feel so passionate about dyslexia and the individuals impacted by it? The answer is easy: they have inspired me with amazing strengths that are often not even noticed or seen as important. The lives of those who have dyslexia could be turned around in an amazing way if we would just help them discover their strengths. Remediation is also vital, but emphasis of what the student can do while working on what they can't yet do is the motivation that can keep them pushing forward.

If you've ever been to a motivational conference, you know the impact it can have. Zig Ziglar is a motivational speaker who is still in great demand after at least four decades. I still remember how contagious his enthusiasm was when attending a conference in the eighties. Most businesses recognize the value of motivation and the effect it has on production. So why has the practice of motivation and encouragement been pushed to a low priority in many of our classrooms, or at least for students who learn differently? One of the biggest contributing factors is that teachers are so consumed with meeting district, state, and global standards that they don't have the energy to deal with the unique strengths and learning styles of each child.

Students need to experience some validated success in order to have the confidence to deal with the difficulties they face. Dyslexia is much more than a reading impairment. It is rooted in a brain-processing difference that creates strengths as well as challenges, and until we fully recognize this, we are doing a great disservice to these individuals.

> Dyslexia associated strengths and challenges are inextricably connected, like home runs and strike-outs in baseball, and dyslexic challenges are best understood as trade-offs made in pursuit of other, larger cognitive gains. (Eide, 2011)

Students are more likely to accept their learning differences if they discover what they can do well. It is as necessary as air is to breathing or water is to quenching thirst. This fact has been validated over and over by those who have dyslexia. "I figured out that if I accepted my disability and worked with my strengths, I really could succeed" (Luke Bornheimer as quoted in Hubbell, 2012)

Previously, we looked at common signs of dyslexia while acknowledging the complexity of individual uniqueness. The same is true of strengths. Even though there are some common strengths, each individual with dyslexia is unique in the way these strengths are exhibited and if they even possess them. While acknowledging individuality, strengths can be broadly characterized into three categories:

- Visual-Spatial / Three-Dimensional / Thinking in Pictures
- Insight / "Get the Gist" Thinkers
- Creativity / Imagination / "Outside-the-Box Thinkers"

We will also explore common career choices that utilize these strengths. And finally, we will look at perseverance, the most important trait that, if possessed, can lead to reaching one's full potential. Perseverance is what motivates us to fight through obstacles, and this is the single trait that has led to such a large number of extremely successful individuals who happen to have dyslexia.

Common Strengths

- **Visual-Spatial / Three-Dimensional / Thinking in Pictures**

Even though the ability to process three-dimensionally is shared by all of us, it is often particularly strong in the dyslexic brain. This strength, also referred to as visual-spatial, is closely related to thinking in pictures. This is one of the most common strengths, and its benefits may account for the high number of dyslexic engineers. But what exactly does it mean to process information in this manner?

> What is visual-spatial processing? It's the ability to locate points in three-dimensional space; perceiving depth; orienting lines in space; understanding geometric relationships; forms and shapes; tracking movements; moving an object over time (which is an incredible complex thing to do—our brains do it well—computers don't); rotating an object; global navigation; and reading a map. I would suggest that most people with dyslexia have a strong visual-spatial channel. (Gordon Sherman as quoted in Hubbell, 2012)

This definition is helpful, but how does it actually make a difference in everyday activities? Imagine what it would be like to have everything that we see in our three-dimensional world recorded on a video camera, stored in our brain, and then forever imprinted in our memories. That is how Anna's mother explained it to me when trying to understand how her husband and two children, all who have dyslexia, process experiences as compared to how her brain processes the same experiences.

The difference became evident when she noticed that Anna remembered, with great visual detail, what she saw at the humane society when picking out their dog, Kinko. After several years had passed, Anna was able to recall the dogs in kennels as they walked down the rows to finally meet Kinko: she remembered the breed and color of all of the animals as she walked past. Likewise, family members who had dyslexia were able to recall details about vacations after several years had passed. Her husband could describe the exact location of an ice-cream factory they visited ten years prior as well as the ten-mile strip leading up to the factory. The video camera in their heads permanently imprint what they see and experience, an ability that most of us don't possess, at least not to this extent.

Children who have strong visual-spatial strengths are easy to pick out in the classroom. They are the ones who like to draw, work on puzzles, create with Legos, build models, and take things apart and put them back together. It saddens me to see these wonderful talents squelched because they don't fit into the curriculum. And further damage is done when these children are expected to spend six hours each day primarily doing academic tasks that are extremely difficult for them with no outlet to do activities they excel in.

There are many career fields that require strong visual-spatial skills. Here are two examples.

> Listen to dyslexic designer Sebastian Bergne: "If I'm designing an object, I know the exact shape in 3-D. I can walk around it in my head before drawing it." (Eide, 2011)

Glenn Bailey is another example of someone with strong visual-spatial skills. He is a Canadian entrepreneur who dropped out of school because of academic problems and is now a very successful businessman.

> One of his many successful ventures has been the development and construction of residential real estate. Glenn described for us how his ability to generate and voluntarily manipulate vivid, lifelike, 3-D visual imagery often helps him in this business. "When I see a property I can instantly construct a new house on it." (Eide, 2011)

There seems to be a disproportionate number of individuals with dyslexia who possess strong visual-spatial strengths, and until we recognize this, children will continue to suffer through school until they are finally set free to explore and develop this talent.

- **Insight / Get the Gist Thinkers**

Students with dyslexia often struggle to read fluently, which typically affects comprehension due to the mental energy required to simply decode the words. However, those with strong insight, are able to get the gist of a passage despite the struggle to read it. I remember being in awe of Justin, from chapter 4, when he could answer the tough questions that required abstract, higher-order thinking skills, after barely being able to decode the passage.

So what does it mean to get the gist?

> Gist is the main point, essence, or overall meaning of a thing, idea, concept, or experience. It's the "rough," coarse, or bird's-eye view, rather than the fine-detail view: the forest rather than the trees. For example, when a telephone or radio message is garbled by static, we use gist detection to determine the context of the message as a whole, then we use this knowledge of context to fill in the details we've missed. (Eide, 2011)

Insight must be nurtured with an environment that is free from stress. It can be easily squelched when the emphasis is on speed and quantity of work. Insight happens when the mind is in a relaxed state, not when forced or hurried.

It can be difficult to distinguish between students who are processing information to gain deeper understanding and those who are simply disengaged.

Unfortunately, increasing demands placed on teachers is causing classrooms to become more regimented with little room for individual student creativity and expression. We have our traditions that continue to emphasize paperpencil, desk-oriented, teacher-dominated, and technology-driven teaching styles, which can work for many. However, this type of environment doesn't allow for those who could bring additional insight and perspective to routine tasks. If students could have access to develop their creativity with time for reflection, their school experiences could be much more positive.

- **Creativity / Imagination/ Thinking Outside the Box**

Schools have been forced to educate our children with less money each year, and music and art programs are often the first to go. The classroom caters to those who learn in a more traditional manner, using primarily auditory and visual senses, with few opportunities for hands-on activities and even fewer opportunities to think creatively and learn through discovery.

Time restraints and the constraints of having to use curriculums "with fidelity", a common expression heard in today's schools, causes teachers to disregard the student who thinks outside the box. This leads to one way to work a problem, one way to answer a question, one way to think. The teacher doesn't have time to consider each student's path of logic when there is a classroom full of distractible students. Teachers often inadvertently squelch the creative thinker, whether because they don't have time or they are busy maintaining order in the classroom. Sometimes it is because the teacher is not following a student's thought process.

> When processing a word or concept, many individuals with dyslexia activate an unusually broad "field" of possible meanings rather than a tightly focused one. As a result, they are less likely to respond first with the primary or most common answers, and more likely to give unusual or creative answers, or a range of possible meanings and relationships. (Eide, 2011)

Usually there is more than one way to complete a task or grasp a new concept. When dealing with a whole classroom of students, teachers often want students to complete their assignments the same way so it is easier to grade, or because it fits the teacher's learning style, or matches the curriculum guidelines. However, if students are allowed to complete tasks using their own strategies, they often will grasp the concept with greater understanding.

Despite the limitations of our educational system, most teachers appreciate and strive to encourage those who think outside the box. Sometimes creativity comes out in a student's writing if educators can get past the numerous spelling, grammar, and structural errors. Emmy award-winning actress Sarah Joy Brown shares the impact one teacher had on her. After getting back a paper that looked like a "war zone" with all of the red marks indicating errors, Sarah was particularly surprised by the big A at the top. When she questioned the teacher, he said, "Because you're really brilliant. You're a great writer, but you're dyslexic. I don't think I should grade you down for that." This had a huge impact on how she perceived herself and her dyslexia. (Hubbell, 2012)

> "Imagination is more important than knowledge. Knowledge is limited. Imagination encircles the world." (Albert Einstein)

Albert Einstein had two completely different experiences when exploring his creativity and imagination. In school, he was simply considered a slow learner; at home he was considered clever, finding fun in building models and mechanical devices.

A question we can all ask ourselves is, *How can we encourage these wonderful strengths in the children we have relationships with?* Some possibilities are giving opportunities to explore and play, voicing questions in everyday experiences, and encouraging students to take the steps to get those questions answered. Encouraging these strengths and their further development can change a life.

Common Career Choices

When individuals with dyslexia discover their strengths, it usually drives their career choice. This is especially true for those who are strong in visual-spatial and creativity skills. If you search the Internet for dyslexic engineers, dyslexic architects, or dyslexic entrepreneurs, you will be inundated with sites.

The career options that are proportionally higher for those with dyslexia are:

Engineers	Designers	Mechanics	Surgeons
Architects	Artists	Electricians	Radiologists
Inventors	Carpenters	Entrepreneurs	Chemists
Physicists	Plumbers	Astronomers	Musicians
Novelists	Filmmakers	Athletes	Computer Specialists

> The high frequency of engineers and archi-
> tects among this group is particularly impressive.
> Together these two professions account for less
> than 6 percent of the college degrees awarded in the
> United States, but they accounted for 25 percent of
> the parents in our survey. (Eide, 2011)

Currently, the emphasis of our education system at the K12 level is on college preparation and being competitive internationally. Students are on the same track with little thought of the individuality of each. Practical skills for life, including financial independence and helping students discover their interests and strengths, are not part of the curriculum of most schools.

Guiding students to the discovery of strengths, and how these strengths can be used to contribute to our society, could make the difference between someone dropping out of school and catching the spirit of becoming a life-long learner. But the biggest indicators of success are perseverance, having a passion for something, and being willing to take risks.

Perseverance / Passion / Risk-Taker

Perseverance, coupled with the drive and passion needed to be a risk-taker, are perhaps the most important traits to possess when faced with any type of disability. Dyslexia is no exception. The day-to-day failures can be met with a defeatist attitude or a fighting spirit of survival. Stories of those who have overcome their obstacles are more numerous than can be shared in one book. However, their stories can shed light on possible potentials hidden in children who are struggling today.

Three well-known individuals whose dyslexia could not keep them down due to perseverance and hard work, may serve as examples of the countless others who have also excelled in life. All three, Jim Carrey, Charles Schwab, and Thomas Edison, fought to overcome their obstacles.

We learned in chapter 6 that Jim Carrey's defense mechanism was to become the class clown; no surprise given he is now a famous comedian. He also developed an amazing memory which led to success in the acting business. But perhaps his true success was catapulted by the hardships. Not only did he have to work around his dyslexia while at school, but at the age of sixteen he had to work an eight-hour night shift in a factory to help his family pay the bills. Jim Carrey's creativity and perseverance were instrumental in his success.

> You can imagine his emotional baggage—the loss of his teen years, feeling intellectually backward, the embarrassment and hardship of poverty. Yet,

perhaps that feeling of inferiority paved the way to his success by making him feel that he had to try harder than others. Jim Carrey used his hard times and setbacks to motivate him to try harder. He could have turned to drugs and drinking. Instead, he channeled his energies to making something special out of his life. As one biographer wrote: "His greatest bursts of creativity were born out of desperation; so was his remarkable willingness to take risks." (My Dyslexia HELP: Success Starts Here– http://dyslexiahelp.umich.edu/success-stories/ jim-carrey)

Just as creativity and perseverance were instrumental in Jim Carrey's success, passion and perseverance led to the success of well-known entrepreneur, Charles Schwab. He is known for revolutionizing the financial industry by opening up the stock market for all. Few know of his dyslexia, and in fact, he didn't have a name for it until his son was diagnosed with it in the 1980s. Now, he is known for more than his good business sense, his ability to think outside the box, and his passion and drive. He and his wife felt so strongly about getting their son the proper support he needed to achieve his dreams, learn in school, and have a healthy self-esteem that they started a resource center for other families. It all started with a passion to help others become advocates for their own children. "You can't just sit back and let things happen, or the kid can be lost," Schwab says, so he and his wife founded *Schwab Learning* "to help the parents of children diagnosed with dyslexia." (dyslexia. yale.edu/schwab)

Schwab elaborates on early experiences in the classroom in a *2003 USA Today* article: "I didn't quit, because I was really good in other things, terrific in math and science and anything that didn't deal with words." Schwab summed up his secret to success by saying, "Passion is the great slayer of adversity. Focus on strengths and what you enjoy."

Thomas Edison is known above all for never giving up in the face of failure. He is the great risk-taker, using his failures to bring us numerous inventions. He is also one of many who was so misunderstood in the school setting that he was seen as a failure. When Edison was six years old, a teacher actually wrote this about him: "He is too stupid to learn." This teacher's assessment of Edison could not be further from the truth, as seen by his advanced scientific thinking as an American inventor. The electric light bulb, the phonograph, and the motion picture camera, to name a few, were among the inventions that required many trial and errors to ultimately lead to success. He was not swayed by repeated failure; instead, it made him the ultimate risk-taker. Edison's life philosophy is summed up in three quotes and are amongst the most inspirational whether we learn best in traditional ways or nontraditional ways.

> Our greatest weakness lies in giving up. The most certain way to succeed is always to try just one more time.

> I have not failed. I've just found 10,000 ways that won't work.

> Genius is one percent inspiration and ninety-nine percent perspiration. (Thomas Edison)

Perseverance is the greatest indicator for achieving dreams. We can persist through almost any obstacle if we possess enough drive and feel enough passion for what we want to achieve. In the face of dyslexia, this is critical. "Free from pencil/paper academics, they thrive. As Woody Allen might say, 'there is life after school.'" (Priscilla L. Vail, *About Dyslexia*).

Myth: You're not dyslexic if you don't reverse letters and numbers.

Busted:

> Many dyslexic children who do not make reversals are often undiagnosed. One frustrated father who was trying to obtain help for his daughter commented, "They say she doesn't have a problem, she just has to work harder and that she can't have dyslexia because she doesn't transpose letters or write backward." (Shaywitz, 2003)

> "For some truly dyslexic children—in our experience roughly one in four—letter reversals can be a much more persistent and important problem." (Eide, 2011)

8

? Dyslexia Can Be Outgrown ?
The Importance of Advocacy

Kristi's Story: Becoming one's own Champion

"I believe that all students should be treated equal. It's not fair to give you extra time if the whole class doesn't also get extra time." Kristi's first-year college professor made it clear that she wasn't going to be swayed by any document stating she had the right to receive accommodations, even if it was a legally binding contract. "Having accommodations is an unfair advantage over the rest of the students," she added. The words hit Kristi in the face like a wet rag as she realized that college was going to be harder than she thought. The class work alone was a challenge due to her dyslexia, and now she feared she would have to jump through all kinds of bureaucratic hoops just to make it through.

Then, fire was added to the hoop when the professor repeatedly made Kristi the butt of negative examples in the weeks following. The defeated feeling turned to anger. She thought about all the prior battles her parents had fought on her behalf. They had been her advocates, fighting to secure the needed academic accommodations throughout elementary and secondary school. And now, facing new barriers all alone, it all felt so unfair.

The seeming insurmountable roadblock, however, awakened her first big leap of growth in learning how to stand up for her own rights. The baton was passing: after years of her mother's advocacy role, Kristi now had to become her own advocate. She had to draw on the wisdom her mother had modeled to move beyond the stalemate she found herself in. Unfortunately, the battle had just begun.

Communication was key. However, informing her teacher that she had dyslexia, making it take longer to complete tests and assignments that involved extensive reading or writing, fell on deaf ears. Showing the necessary documentation which would allow her the accommodation of extra time was rejected. But Kristi's realization that the way she was treated was a form of discrimination became the pivotal point.

Since Kristi hit a roadblock with her teacher, she took the issue to the Dean of Education. The word that opened the door to action was *discrimination*. The rights of students with disabilities are protected by the Rehabilitation Act of 1973, under Section 504. It is an antidiscrimination, civil rights statute that requires the needs of students with disabilities to be met as adequately as the needs of the nondisabled are met. This allows any student with a disability, including dyslexia, to be allowed access to the same education if they are "otherwise qualified" and have the desire to complete the work with tools and accommodations to make access possible. When Kristi did not qualify for special education services in elementary school, her mother took the initiative to get her a 504 Plan. This became the stimulus for change then, and now as she stood before the dean.

Communication resulted in an assurance that the 504 Plan would be followed, allowing her extra time to complete tests and assignments as needed. It also led to a temporary leave of absence for the teacher who believed treating students equally meant everyone should learn and process the same way. Kristi was learning how to stand up for herself, a skill that will undoubtedly bring lifelong benefits.

When did the need for advocacy begin for Kristi? It began with her mom's recognition of a subtle difference in her daughter when she was very young. The family would engage in rhyming games while traveling, and when family members took turns rhyming words such as *cat* and *hat*, or *car* and *bar*, Kristi couldn't do it. Difficulty with rhyming is a big red flag for dyslexia. Also, when she read aloud at home, she often inserted the wrong sound in words; for example, *gand* for *sand*, another indicator of dyslexia.

When Kristi's mom saw these little differences, she didn't automatically think dyslexia. But as she saw her daughter struggle in school, she knew she had to do something. Kristi's teachers had other students with more serious learning issues, so with little understanding and support at school, the family decided to take her to a pediatrician to discuss concerns. Even though many doctors are not educated on the subject of dyslexia, the physician the family chose was known for his expertise. He formally diagnosed Kristi with dyslexia.

With official paperwork in hand, Mom began educating the educators. In addition, she heeded the doctor's recommendation to get Kristi into a tutoring program that uses the Orton-Gillingham approach. The decision to do whatever it took to help alleviate her academic frustration brought me into the picture.

I was privileged to work with Kristi for three years. We worked together three hours each week and completed the Alphabetic Phonics Program just prior to attending middle school. Some of the aspects of remediation can be tedious and repetitive, so for an occasional break in the normal routine, Kristi would tackle brainteasers to help boost her already apparent strengths. One particular 3-D brainteaser has only been solved by Kristi. I've asked others to try to solve the same puzzle, and none have been successful. Unfortunately, the answer key is long gone, and I'm still baffled as to how she did it. Intelligence is so much deeper than the ability to read fluently, as evidenced by Kristi.

Kristi not only has strong visual-spatial strengths, but she also has strong social skills. Being socially savvy, with a compromising attitude, and hard work ethic cause teachers to want to help her through the tough tasks. When schoolwork becomes difficult, Kristi figures it out by other means and doesn't give up.

Despite scores demonstrating that Kristi was college ready, dyslexia is not outgrown. Therefore, accommodations are extremely helpful, given the heavy load of reading that many classes require as well as the accompanying essays, research papers, and other writing assignments. Accommodations don't make the work less, but they do make it more manageable.

Many dyslexic college students excel in the overall college process if they discover tools and tricks that allow them to use their learning style, and if they take advantage of accommodations, such as being allowed extra time. In chapter 9, Shaun and Drayton share some of their tips to success.

On her growth curve to self-advocacy, Kristi is learning college survival depends on learning which teachers are accommodating, and which ones are not. She then enrolls in classes where open communication with instructors is encouraged. Her observation of her first college conflict was, "If one teacher thinks this way, there are probably others."

Kristi aspires to become a teacher. She feels her struggles in the classroom can make her a better teacher with more empathy for students grappling with learning differences. Also, Kristi has had to learn tasks by breaking them down into smaller steps, which could be a great asset in teaching others.

Kristi's life struggles are leading her to maturity. They are helping her gain a more well-rounded perspective on life as she is learning how to advocate for herself. And yet, the end result will be so much more than a college diploma. She is learning valuable communication and negotiating skills necessary for life and work relationships. These are skills that everyone needs though not everyone possesses. These are skills that make one wise not just educated. Gaining the skills to become one's own advocate are the building blocks for independence and happiness. And Kristi is well on her way to both!

Becoming Your Own Advocate or the Advocate of Another

> All of us are different. If someone rises to the occasion of their disability and conquers it, instead of using it as an excuse, I have huge respect for him or her. You are the master of your own ship. Steer it! You are the one who has to go out there and claim your own future. (Nelsan Ellis)

Advocacy for the dyslexic student is as necessary as a life preserver is to someone drowning. With it they can survive, and without it they can sink beneath the murky waters of confusion. The role of advocate typically falls to a parent although anyone with knowledge of dyslexia can take on this important lifesaving job. I fell into this role when I finally realized I did not have the tools necessary to teach this mysterious group of children, whom I didn't yet have a name for. Dyslexia was not yet part of my educational jargon, but I did recognize these children as bright despite the fact that they could not read and write like their peers.

It was after my training at the Fundamental Learning Center that I recognized the possibility that perhaps my own brother may have had dyslexia. This possibility and realizing that dyslexia is what plagued several of my students was what motivated me to get involved and become another voice of advocacy.

Why is advocacy so important? In most schools, there is no one to speak on behalf of the dyslexic child due to a general lack of knowledge. Also in the classroom, the ratio is usually one teacher to approximately thirty students, making giving the dyslexic student individual attention very difficult. Teachers have to prioritize their energy, which typically leaves the dyslexic child to fall by the wayside.

> It eventually dawns on parents intuitively that if they leave their child in an unhealthy situation much longer without intervening, they will be cooperating in a type of educational and emotional neglect. It is a harsh realization that public school officials see a child's educational need as a threat to policy, to personnel, to professional development budgets, to administrative versus citizen control, to the status quo of testing and identifying students at risk, to the distribution of government money, and to perceived real estate values versus percentages of district students with learning challenges. (Carol Hill as quoted in Hubbell, 2012)

So what do students with dyslexia need from us in order to maneuver through school and life? Steps of advocacy can be broken down into six steps: become knowledgeable, push for early intervention, give encouragement, get remediation, be persistence, and get involved in policy change. In addition to these six steps we will look at accommodations and assistive technology tools that can help students become successful in the classroom and beyond, the need for community, and how to get the right support in schools. Eventually, students can be taught to advocate for themselves, but in the beginning, they need someone else to have their back.

Steps of Advocacy

Step 1: Become Knowledgeable

Read, read, read! And if reading is difficult, find the audio versions of books and articles on the subject of dyslexia. A good start is the references listed at the end of this book. Explore the Internet with caution. There are many philosophies and suggested strategies floating around on the Internet, some even endorsed in our schools. However, many of these have no research to back them up. As we saw in chapter 3, studies throughout the last century have given us evidence-based strategies.

Many good resources emphasize the positive aspects of dyslexia with encouraging success stories to bring hope. Seeing the positives while in the midst of the struggles can be critical to both the dyslexic individual and those who love them.

Step 2: Push for Early Intervention

Teachers want to offer encouragement to worried parents, so one of the most common encouragements that they give is, "I'm sure he's just a late bloomer. Let's just wait and I'm sure he'll catch up." Unfortunately, this often is not the case. It is more likely that the child requires different teaching techniques, and the best time to intervene is at a young age when the brain is more pliable.

Most don't want to go against the advice of someone in authority, and they want to believe the advice that their child will outgrow their academic difficulties. But if we don't address issues early, the intervention needed can take much longer, and there can be irrevocable damage to a child's self-esteem. Only when we are proactive, doing whatever it takes to assure early identification, can the problem be tackled before it becomes a big issue.

Step 3: Encourage, Encourage, Encourage!

If a child doesn't have someone who believes in him, he will stop believing in himself. Discouragement can be the biggest hindrance to learning. It is as important to help a child see they have worth and help them discover their strengths as it is to teach them to master reading, writing, and math.

> When Sarah had trouble in school, I immediately recognized what it was all about and I said, "I will never allow my child to feel stupid like I did." It was a fight all through her years in school, making her feel special, not stupid, not letting her think she had a disease, but a gift. Still, she was ridiculed, she was humiliated, and I would have to take her out of one school and put her in another. We worked together to get her through school. (Cary Spier as quoted in Hubbell, 2012)

Whoopi Goldberg credits her mother with helping her to believe in herself. According to paperwork, Whoopi was "retarded" with a dyslexia diagnosis coming much later. On the contrary, Whoopi had extraordinary gifts, and her mother's encouragement helped her through the tough years of "feeling as if she wasn't grasping anything taught in the classroom." Whoopi says, "I knew I wasn't stupid, and I knew I wasn't dumb. My mother told me that." She adds, "Normal is nothing more than a cycle on a washing machine." (http://www.dyslexia-reading-well.com/whoopi-goldberg.html)

Teachers have so much on their plate, so it becomes a matter of prioritizing. Building relationships with students can make the difference between a student's success or failure. We have to get their attention with positivity if we want them to learn.

> Every single student brings hundreds of stories with them to school. Those stories are the framework for their lives and teachers must value and honor students' backgrounds, families, cultures and economic situations. It is not just the stories students BRING TO school; it is the stories that great teachers PULL OUT of them—their dreams, their hopes, their goals. Outstanding teachers truly understand what makes their students tick. (Laughlin, 2015)

Step 4: Get Remediation

Currently getting the right remediation is only possible for some. This option is dependent on where you live and whether you can afford it. For those who want to pursue remediation, you can either find a school or hire a therapist that provides specialized instruction. Some parents and grandparents have even committed to getting the training necessary to provide needed instruction themselves.

If you find yourself in a school that either does not acknowledge dyslexia or lumps everyone with disabilities into one group, search out schools, dyslexia centers, and other community resources in your area that can provide the right kind of help. Dyslexia Reading Well has a list of schools and other resources on their website: http://www.dyslexia-reading-well.com/schools-for-dyslexia-united-states.html.

> We sent Jo'Von to a small independent school in Connecticut. It made all the difference in the world. She was a flower waiting to come alive and bloom. She moved up three grade levels in reading in one year because she was able to utilize the techniques they taught her. There, she began to develop the self-confidence to stand on her own two feet. (Voncile Wright as quoted in Hubbell, 2012)

If you decide you want to hire a therapist to provide the appropriate instruction, the best scenario is to find someone who has been trained through an accredited organization such as the International Multisensory Structured Language Council (IMSLEC). The Academic Language Therapy Association (ALTA) provides a list of certified therapists in each state. (www.altaread.org)

Step 5: Be Persistent, Don't Give Up!

When it comes to dyslexia, the need for advocacy doesn't end until we can eventually teach the individual with dyslexia to advocate for themselves. Dyslexia is so misunderstood in our society that we must be persistent in educating those who have no experience or knowledge of it. Those who work with our dyslexic children, whether it be teachers, principals, or coaches, typically know very little about dyslexia.

It takes persistence to go to each group of educators, year after year, and tell them about your dyslexic child's needs, especially when it places additional demands on their time and attention. You may not see or hear the collective sighs of, *Here she comes again!* but you have to decide what is more important—the dyslexic child or the overwhelmed teacher.

> I'm sure I've been very annoying, and I don't like being like this. I would much rather be in the back seat and be more helpful, but sometimes you have to be forceful. I've tried to bring to the school certain programs I've found through the IDA, and this has fallen on deaf ears. (Diana Naples as quoted in Hubbell, 2012)

The role of advocate often falls in the parent's lap, and they're in it for the long haul. Many can pass it on to the child by the time they're in college, but even that is not a guarantee as we saw in Cooper's story. If his mom hadn't intervened, he wouldn't have graduated without much added expense and time. Ultimately, the dyslexic individual must learn to communicate what they need in school and in the workforce. This isn't always easy as we see from Elisha's experience.

> My most difficult experience in college is when I have to drop a class. I was too ashamed to ask for help at first, and at one point a professor suggested that I drop his course before it brought my GPA down. I was disappointed with myself, but from then on, I decided to ask for help when I needed it, even though that meant putting my pride aside. That's a small price to pay when the reward is a bright future. (Elisha Wenzela as quoted in Hubbell, 2012)

Persistence is often the biggest contributor to success. After listening to stories and reading articles about the many dyslexics who have "made it," the underlying trait throughout their stories has been the fact that they didn't give up. They kept persisting even when it was hard. And they found that the benefits far outweighed any embarrassment or shame they occasionally felt when having to ask for help.

Step 6: Get Involved with Policy Change

When parents of dyslexic children get together, they often find they share similar experiences, especially when trying to get help for their child in the public school system. This is how Decoding Dyslexia-NJ began. It began in October of 2011 as a group of eight New Jersey parents discovered they had a lot in common. "We shared our stories, our struggles, our heart breaks and our frustrations and anger about trying to help our dyslexic children and getting nowhere within our public schools....By the end of the day, we declared that someone should do something to help other parents like us and to fix the system. We decided that collectively, maybe we could be that someone." The group of eight started Decoding Dyslexia–NJ, and there are now several branches located across America. Their purpose statement gives us a glimpse of what can happen when people join together.

> Decoding Dyslexia is a network of parent-led grass-roots movements across the country concerned with the limited access to educational interventions for dyslexia within the public education system. We aim to raise dyslexia awareness, empower families

to support their children and inform policy-makers on best practices to identify, remediate and support students with dyslexia.

We are advocating for the following policy goals:

- A universal definition and understanding of "dyslexia" in the state education code
- Mandatory teacher training on dyslexia, its warning signs and appropriate intervention strategies
- Mandatory early screening tests for dyslexia
- Mandatory dyslexia remediation programs, which can be accessed by both general and special education populations
- Access to appropriate "assistive technologies" in the public school setting for students with dyslexia

Each state organizes and inspires its own local movement by networking with families and professionals to gain support for the Decoding Dyslexia mission. We recognize the power of the collective parent voice and work diligently to encourage individuals and organizations to partner and collaborate in the best interest of supporting families and advancing services for dyslexics.

> I really believe parents are the key to changing
> policy. If parents get angry enough and organize in
> a positive way that empowers them to believe they
> can bring about change, I think that would send
> the message to our policy makers, our legislators,
> and our leaders that we are not going to stand for
> this anymore. We have too many kids in pain who
> are going to struggle their whole lives because they
> didn't learn to read in first grade. (Margie Gillis as
> quoted in Hubbell, 2012)

Given the significant lack of knowledge concerning dyslexia throughout our society, politicians also need to be educated. According to Linda Selvin, politicians need to know
"it's not brain surgery, it's a technique. And they can save
lots of money, educate many more children, and create a
much more dynamic work force with early intervention. It
is to their benefit. And it benefits all of us." (Hubbell, 2012)

Accommodations and Assistive Technology

Imagine if we refused to give a child who is nearsighted
glasses, or denied the child with a hearing loss a hearing
aid. Sounds absurd, right? How is that different from refusing to give a child who is a slow processor extra time on
exams? Is speed really what we want to test? Many are so

concerned with not giving anyone an unfair advantage that we have lost sight of individuality, just another indication of trying to fit everything neat and tidy into a black-and-white viewpoint. Allowing students to have accommodations and / or assistive technology simply helps students to manage and have access to learning.

Helping children achieve their full potential should be the ultimate goal in school and beyond. Children with learning differences need to be exposed to resources and tools that allow for unique learning styles, and with ever-increasing technology, the opportunities are limitless. It can make the difference between success and failure, as we see by Blake Charlton's experience.

> As Blake Charlton recalled of his middle school years, "I was given a calculator and spell-check for everything, and almost overnight I went from just barely passing my exams to being very far up on the curve." (Eide, 2011)

Accommodations are changes made to the school environment, curriculum, or equipment that helps a student overcome or work around a disability, giving them access to content and the ability to complete assigned tasks. Accommodations can include, but are not limited to: extra time allowance, shortened assignments, working in a small group or one on one with teacher, test questions read aloud, allowing answers to be given orally or dictated, use of a word processor for written work, and providing audiotaped lectures or books.

Assistive technology is any tool that helps students with disabilities do things more quickly, easily, or independently. It allows them to use more time to master both strengths and weaknesses. We've already discussed the importance of remediation, but there is a point when students need the tools necessary to allow their higher level thinking skills to flourish. Most students respond to remediation, but for some, especially for the older student, time can be better spent teaching them how to use assistive technology in order to gain more independence. This is not to discount remediation for the older student just to prioritize the order of implementation.

Ben Foss is a great proponent of giving students the right accommodations. When he gave up on the idea of ever learning to read, he turned to assistive technology and educational accommodations to help him reach his goals. This was how he was able to earn his bachelor's and master's degrees and get a combined JD/MBA from Stanford. Ben describes accommodations as "interventions that get you out of unproductive activities and into productive ones. Accommodations are a ramp for a wheelchair. They're a modification to a process that is still true to the end goal:

the test is still the test, and the knowledge is still the knowledge, but accommodations provide a different way to gain access to it." (Eide, 2011)

There are many forms of assistive technology that can be beneficial to the student with dyslexia, but here are some of the more popular:

- Audiobook—a recording of a text being read. A reading of the complete text is noted as "unabridged," while readings of a reduced version is labeled as "abridged."
- Livescribe smartpen—a ballpoint pen with an embedded computer and digital audio recorder. When used with Anoto digital paper, it records what it writes for later uploading to a computer and synchronizes those notes with any audio it has recorded. This allows users to replay portions of a recording by tapping on the notes they were taking at the time the recording was made.
- Dragon Naturally Speaking for PC/Dragon Dictate for Mac—a voice recognition program that allows you to dictate your ideas and watch your words appear on the computer screen. It can be used for those who have word retrieval difficulties, writing weaknesses, or problems committing ideas to paper in a timely fashion.

- iPad 3 Speech to Text Option—the microphone icon on its keyboard offers students the opportunity to generate text through their voices instead of typing.
- Word processors with text predict—students who find difficulty with the physical act of handwriting or spelling and reading can express their creativity without limitations.

Ben's use of audio books while pursuing his law degree worked for him. He says, "I never touched a book in law school. I learned to abandon reading. That was the approach that allowed me to keep up with all the assignments. I chose a totally different road than most students, because for me going through the book road was like inching over an unpaved road, while going through my alternative formats was like speeding down the autobahn." Ben suggests Learning Ally (www.learningally.org) as a resource to search for recorded text.

A valuable tool for all ages is exposure to audio books. Children are naturally curious and their interest in some topics may require text that is above their reading level. It is important to have access to recorded books that give them that exposure. Recorded text can accomplish a variety of purposes. It can be used to further reinforce decodable reading, or text that uses words that can be phonetically sounded out or specialized to help with spelling. Recorded text can be used to increase vocabulary or support comprehensive skills since decodable texts are not as complex. Audio books can open a whole world to students who otherwise are wasting time away in frustration.

In the next chapter, Shaun shares a technique he used while in college. When he couldn't find required reading in the audio format, he would tear pages out of his textbooks and have them digitalized so he could listen to them on his computer. This is just one example of creative measures to survive college.

> "If you had a blind child who was trying to learn to read, you would never yell at him and say that he could see better if he worked harder at it. You would teach him to use Braille, and let him access books that way." (Hubbell, 2012)

The Need for Knowledge and Community

When we feel all alone in our troubles, feelings of isolation can be overwhelming. Our society has support groups for every life scenario, and individuals with dyslexia need the same support. Disability rights advocate, Ben Foss, speaks to how liberating and empowering it is when fellow dyslexic individuals have opportunities to share their experiences.

> When you meet another dyslexic, it's like you're immigrants meeting in a new land. You instantly know important things about each other, and that experience of being from the same country is incredibly powerful. (Ben Foss as quoted in Eide, 2011)

When children see that they can't do what others do so easily, their inner voice goes one of two ways: they can sink into a defeatist *I'm stupid* mentality, or their inner voice can express the confusion of *I know I'm smart, so why don't I get this?*

It doesn't matter which voice they tend to listen to; if they have support, negative thinking can turn positive and they can overcome. Giving the dyslexic child facts about how their brain processes, affording them both strengths and weaknesses, can change the day-to-day internal dialogue

The need for community for those with dyslexia is priceless. Feelings of isolation and the ever-looming dread of being different can be stopped in its tracks. Within community, helpful strategies and resources can be shared that extend beyond the benefits of relationships being built.

Project Eye-to-Eye, a mentoring movement for different thinkers, is a great resource for college-bound youth with learning challenges. It began because of two talented individuals who saw the need for community. David Flink, author of *Thinking Differently*, *An Inspiring Guide for Children with Learning Disabilities*, and Jonathan Mooney, author of *Learning Outside the Lines*, founded Project Eye-to-Eye. "We fulfill our mission by supporting and growing a network of youth mentoring programs run by and for those with learning differences, and by organizing advocates to support the full inclusion of people with learning disabilities and ADHD in all aspects of society."

It may be helpful to also look at some of the structure within our K-12 schools to give support to our dyslexic students and how we can pursue additional support. Do we continue to just tell them we're sorry they feel the way they do, or do we offer support? With an increasing amount of resources and information on dyslexia, there is only one good answer. Ignoring their pleas for help, whether spoken or unspoken, is neglectful to say the least.

How to get Support in School

When students struggle to learn and keep pace with their classmates, a teacher or parent can request a comprehensive evaluation to determine eligibility for special education services. Students must meet three criteria to be eligible: they must have a disability or disabilities, the disability/disabilities have to adversely affect educational performance, and the student's unique needs cannot be addressed through education in general education classes alone.

Students with dyslexia typically meet all three criteria; however, schools have adopted the 3-Tier Model of Educational Intervention as a means of meeting individual student needs within the classroom. RTI Action Network works at implementing Response to Intervention nationwide with three levels of intervention and instruction.

Tier 1: **High-Quality Classroom Instruction, Screening, and Group Interventions**

Tier 2: **Targeted Interventions**

Tier 3: **Intensive Interventions and Comprehensive Evaluation**

Ideally, students with dyslexia would receive remediation in our schools under Tier 2 or Tier 3. However, in my experience, it is not happening in most schools, and research-based strategies and the five components to reading instruction discussed in chapter 3 are either oversimplified or ignored. While it seems unfair to the one in five students left to struggle, I also recognize that within the current structure of the classroom, meeting all students' needs is an overwhelming task. Teachers have so much on their plates just dealing with the normal day-to-day demands. Again, it is usually not a teacher problem, it is a system problem.

If a student does not qualify for special education, and they are not getting support in the classroom through the 3-Tier Model, families can ask for accommodations with a 504 Plan. Kristi's family initiated the paperwork for a 504 plan when she did not qualify for special education services, and it was instrumental in receiving accommodations throughout her schooling, including college.

There is a great deal of confusion on what a 504 Plan is and how to implement one. Because it is separate from special education, it is usually up to the principal or a 504 committee and the parent to write up a plan. If the school does not have the necessary paperwork, the State Department of Education can be contacted for more information and the needed forms. The 504 Plan gives the student rights to the same education as others if they are "otherwise qualified." In other words, the student must demonstrate they are qualified to do something before the presence of a disability. It allows them access to accommodations and/or assistive technology to make participation in any program or activity possible. Implementation of a 504 plan is often initiated by a parent, but anyone wishing to assure a student's full access to their educational needs can get the ball rolling.

Parents have to become very proactive when it comes to making sure the plan is followed. The information and paperwork can get lost in the myriad of other demands, making it necessary for the parent to bring it to the attention of every teacher and administrator, every school year.

Whether we're talking about special education, the 3-Tier Model, or a 504 Plan, the goal of each is to give students educational strategies, interventions, accommodations, and/or assistive technologies to give access to quality education. It is evident that schools are striving to provide quality education; now is the time to take action on behalf of those with dyslexia. We must address the student's need for remediation designed for their specific learning disability, their need for appropriate accommodations and assistive technology, and the educator's need for a better understanding of students with dyslexia.

In Summary

Nelsan Ellis tells us that if we conquer our disability, it is like mastering our own ship. "Steer it," he says. Become your own advocate and advocate for others by throwing out life preservers. These life preservers can make all the difference. Accommodations, assistive technology, support through community and within our schools, gaining knowledge and understanding of dyslexia, assuring early intervention, encouragement, remediation, persistence in the process, and getting involved with policy change can make the difference between sinking or swimming. And the effects are felt for a life.

I wish I could offer some or all of these lifelines to my brother. Things might have turned out differently for him; he might still be with us. But it's never too late for the living.

Myth: Children outgrow dyslexia.
Busted:

> Dyslexia's cognitive and processing pattern appears stable across the lifespan, (Wolf & Bowers, 1999)

> Dyslexia isn't for a moment, it's for a lifetime. Some people in our lives don't believe dyslexia is real or are uncomfortable talking dyslexia. Some think it's like catching a cold, a minor struggle to get past and get over. (Parent of Dyslexic Child).

9

? Dyslexics Can't Go to College ?

Knowing Yourself Leads to Success

Shaun and Drayton: Persevering into College and Beyond

Shaun's Story

For seventeen years, Shaun lived without knowing he had dyslexia. School year after school year, he struggled with tasks that most students found doable. After learning he had dyslexia, Shaun says, "I had no idea what the term meant, but I remember feeling a brief moment of shame, followed by a sense of calm and relief."

The diagnosis helped him see his past in a new light. It gave a name to his realities and a sense that his struggles weren't random. On one hand, if he had known from the start about his diagnosis, life would have been easier for him. On the other hand, he realizes that the struggles gave him the stamina to finish a law degree.

Ironically, even as dyslexia made learning in school a mixture of drudgery and panic, he had a thirst for learning outside of the classroom. "Every toy I owned inevitably met its end as the result of curiosity and a screwdriver," he says. "Access to the Internet only accelerated my information addiction. Yet each morning I woke up miserable at the realization I had to go to school. No matter how smart I may have felt, for five days each week I struggled to keep pace with my classes."

What's the typical path for those like Shaun who struggle to keep the pace? One, they are placed in special education if testing shows enough of a discrepancy between their performance and intelligence. Or two, they are placed in a remedial reading group. The latter was the case for Shaun, which only increased his feelings of not belonging.

The concern over the possibility of not graduating from high school was a breaking point for both Shaun and his mom and propelled them to make needed changes. After briefly being homeschooled, he returned to public school and then was forced to attend night school in order to raise his grades enough to graduate. But Shaun says, "Fortunately for me, somewhere in the chaos of my final high school years, my mom was as desperate as I to find a solution." That solution came in the form of a diagnosis of dyslexia. "Learning more about dyslexia allowed me to learn more about myself," he said.

With this knowledge came the kind of thinking that would pull Shaun through college and motivate him to develop the tools necessary to finish law school. "The most valuable thing I learned was how to accept my weaknesses and have more faith in my strengths," he says. Shaun describes himself as a visual-spatial thinker, which is evident in his notes looking more like pictures, diagrams, and maps than words. He calls it his infographics and mind maps or his way of tricking his creative side to memorize material for finals. In some classes, Shaun uses his illustrations and doodles to help understand concepts. He actively searches for methods that work for him instead of conforming to the "normal way" of studying and learning. His ability to "problem-solve, troubleshoot, and develop ideas by drawing them out first in (his) head, then on paper and whiteboards, in seeming chaos" led to success. And school has actually become enjoyable for him.

Shaun also discovered that accepting his need for academic accommodations was necessary for success. He had to push through the fear that it would alienate him from his peers. He elaborates, "People are generally more accepting of disabilities with physical manifestations—whether as simple as glasses or as severe as wheelchairs—than ones they do not see or understand." Some of Shaun's tips that have helped him get through college are:

- Reading assigned material twice–once line by line using a note card to keep eyes from jumping, and one or more times with a highlighter and pens to mark in the margins.
- Getting audio lectures and listening to them at any spare moment, such as when stuck in traffic.
- Converting notes into mind maps and illustrations and covering walls with them to study for exams.
- If available, getting text in audio format; if not, take apart the textbook in order to have pages digitized, which allow it to be read by computer.
- Watching online tutorials and YouTube videos for more difficult content, using pause and rewind options.

If Shaun didn't have the perseverance and drive to push himself beyond the average expectations, he would not have made it through high school let alone college and law school. His feelings that he was not made for school have been confirmed over the years yet he made it work. He says, "Schools have evolved through tradition and standardization to accommodate statistically ordinary students. As a result, students with any degree of an unconventional way of learning style are forced to adapt or fail." His choice to adapt has been a constant uphill battle but worth it in his eyes.

Shaun wants to share his story because he wants to have an impact in improving things for others with dyslexia. He wants them to have the knowledge that he received late in his schooling, almost too late. Shaun has advice for other students with dyslexia that comes from his personal experiences. He encourages others to:

- Figure out who you are and embrace it.
- Few may ever understand you, and many others may trivialize your struggles, but only you need to understand you.
- Find your strengths and bring them into every aspect of your life and studies no matter how odd or unusual they may be.
- Be aware of your weaknesses and actively look for alternative methods to reach the same goal even if they appear a bit out of the way.
- Most of all, though, find a foundation of support from others.

"Personally, I would have never made it beyond high school without my mom who believed in me more than I believed in myself," he says. "Reaching out to other professionals with dyslexia and learning disabilities also provided me with an invaluable source of encouragement and advice." Discovering that his learning differences were due to dyslexia was the stimulus to self-acceptance, but having the stamina to push through when it was tough has been the key to success.

Drayton's Story

Unlike Shaun, Drayton, who is pursuing a chemical engineering degree, was diagnosed with dyslexia in the first grade. Although their stories may be similar in some aspects, having early knowledge of dyslexia versus no knowledge until the end of K-12 schooling, distinguishes the two. They both have the persistence and drive needed to reach their goals despite similar struggles, yet an early diagnosis and knowledge of dyslexia brought a sense of acceptance at a much younger age for Drayton.

Chemical engineering is one of the most difficult fields of study and is a lofty goal in light of the challenges of dyslexia and ADHD. But early memories shared by Drayton's mom made his chosen major quite obvious. "What in the world is in my freezer?" Mom questioned Drayton, the likely culprit. So what was in the freezer? He was continually experimenting with mixing and inventing things, so it was not uncommon to find odd things all over the house, including in the freezer. Mom recalls seeing inflated balloons in the freezer after Drayton poured different liquids in them, inflated and tied them, then froze them to see what, if anything, would happen. His creative, inventive nature emerged on a regular basis. A particularly humorous creation was his diagram of a veterinarian clinic waiting room with elaborate, fun gizmos for each animal as they waited. Life was never dull when Drayton was around.

Both Drayton and Shaun have creative, curious natures, which is a great asset in college and in their careers to come, but Drayton's early diagnosis gave him a notable advantage early in his life. Drayton's mom is also dyslexic, and her experience and training in the Orton-Gillingham approach as an adult helped her to identify signs in her son at a young age. Recognizing the signs was also confirmed by Drayton's first grade teacher, who said, "He wouldn't make it!" At the first conference, Mom was told he would probably have to repeat first grade, so when he soared ahead of his classmates in reading by the end of the school year, his teacher was amazed. Drayton's mom started his therapy using Reading Readiness when he was four years old, and Alphabetic Phonics when he was in the first grade, at which time he also received an official diagnosis. As a result, he did not suffer some of the struggles that Shaun endured. He says, "Dyslexia can be a crippling disability if you don't get help. I got help early, so it hasn't been as crippling for me."

Even though Drayton learned of his dyslexia early, he still struggled. "I always hated school, because I was not good at it," he says. "It took a lot of motivation just to do the everyday tasks." He recognizes it could have been much worse since early remediation brought him to an eighth grade reading level by the time he was in the fourth grade. However, writing and spelling were still huge stumbling blocks. That and his ADHD caused him to dread every day. Mom's response was to homeschool him for seventh and eighth grade, using the Multisensory Reading and Spelling program. By the time he entered high school, his writing and spelling were on grade level.

Despite conquering the academic skills necessary for success, Drayton felt like a fish out of water in high school since the format of school conflicted with his learning style. Issues related to ADHD and the limitations placed on students to express visual-spatial and creative strengths made for daily dread and boredom. "Organizing eight classes was also a nightmare. Fewer classes each semester in college are a plus."

Drayton is currently in college pursuing a dual degree in chemical engineering and petroleum engineering. His fascination with science, which began before ever attending school, is alive and well. He spent his first three years of rigorous discipline at Kansas State University, and then in the fall of 2015, he transferred to the University of Kansas to complete his final two years. The decision to change schools came with a recognition of how he learns best. Drayton says, "Daily lectures are worthless for me. I have to figure it out on my own." For this reason, he decided to search out programs that would better fit his learning style. He found a better option for him at University of Kansas since their lectures can be done online followed by classes that meet in small groups to work on projects and problem-solving related to the lecture topic. It doesn't matter how old the student is, finding the right school can make all the difference.

He is finding his chosen course of study quite a challenge due to a combination of the difficult course of study— "many students get weeded out really early"—as well as his ADHD. Fortunately for Drayton, however, he feels he has the academic skills necessary to compensate for his dyslexia despite some characteristics that typically never leave those with dyslexia.

A common trait that never fully goes away is word retrieval. When having conversations, he still has difficulty coming up with the right word, and he confuses words that sound similar, as the following shared memory can attest to.

> While sitting in church, the preacher said, "I'm pleased to announce that we have 1000 new people in seminary." Drayton gasps and whispers to his mom, "I can't believe he would say that!" "Say what?"

mom replies. "He just said he's happy that there are 1000 new people in the cemetery!!"

Drayton is no stranger to "hard" and to less-than-stellar grades, although this is helping him persevere through when others quit. In elementary, middle school, and high school, he had to be okay with occasional Cs and Ds. So now in college, he is better able to accept occasional failures. He says, "The ones who drop out, or change majors, aren't used to failure. They think that if they can't maintain As and Bs, then it's too hard, and they quit."

Despite his being okay with okay, Drayton says he can be a perfectionist too, "but not when it comes to recognizing that some things are just more difficult due to dyslexia and ADHD." He makes himself emphasize persistence over perfection. This is where having an understanding of both his strengths and weaknesses has been helpful. Knowing yourself can be just the ticket needed to push through when the going gets tough.

Drayton has a 504 Plan, which stipulates that he can have extra time, if needed, when taking tests. This accommodation has made a big difference, beginning with taking admissions tests. He had a top score of thirty-six on the English portion of the ACT. And in college classes, he takes advantage of asking for extra time when he feels he needs it.

In Drayton's opinion, college is better than high school in a couple ways. First, it's been easier to find others with similar interests in college. In high school, there was an overall lack of motivation; in college, it is easier to find others who are motivated, which in turn motivates him. It is this attitude that is causing Drayton to strive to complete his course work in as few years as possible, even though it takes a tremendous amount of time, leaving him little time for a social life. Secondly, he finds having fewer classes to organize as helpful: four classes as compared to juggling eight classes in high school.

Focusing on reaching one goal at a time is giving Drayton the stamina needed to succeed. He doesn't have time for hobbies, but cherishes the rare bits of downtime when he can hang out with friends. "My main goal now is to get my degree," he says. "It is taking all my energy just to get through college."

Both Shaun and Drayton pushed past the unhappiness of elementary and secondary school with its rigid routines that did not fit them. They persevered in their younger years—the daily watching of the clock for when they would be set free from the classroom. And because of that, they are now watching with anticipation how the realization of their dreams will lead to fulfillment.

Labels: Helpful or Hurtful

By freshman year in high school, I was being taught how to fill out checks and job applications for McDonalds. When I'd ask my special education teacher why I had to continue to do this work, she said that it was to prepare myself for life after high school. I told her I was going to go to college. She told me that maybe I should consider that college was not for me. I had been thinking about college ever since I was five years old. That summer, I came to the Forman School and succeeded academically for the first time. Labels are funny things–we all have more than one. Yes, I have the dyslexia label, but I also have the labels of professor, daughter, scientist, sister, teacher, wife, and mother. Labels are just something that describe one aspect about ourselves. (Annette Jenner as quoted in Hubbell, 2012)

Labels are found in all walks of life. They are what define us, and can either be helpful or hurtful. We label or define ourselves and others by physical and personality traits as well as how we learn. How we perceive ourselves determines who we become. Dyslexia is one of the most misunderstood labels not only in our schools but also in our society as a whole, and until it is better understood, those with dyslexia are hurt.

Over the years, harmful labels such as *retarded* or *lazy* have been attached to those with dyslexia, perceptions that stem from ignorance. Children are more perceptive than we give them credit for, and when they see that they are not learning the same as their peers, the labels are self-inflicted.

On the other hand, receiving the label of dyslexia, when it comes with accurate information can have life-changing effects. A diagnosis of dyslexia should lead to taking appropriate steps to address specific educational needs, as well as giving the individual and those who work with him or her information that can help with acceptance and appreciation for their unique way of thinking. Currently, public schools in most states give dyslexic children the label of Specific Learning Disability, which is too broad to be helpful. It doesn't tell us of their need for direct and explicit, systematic, multisensory, phonetic-based instruction nor does it speak to the accompanying strengths often associated with dyslexia.

Children know when something is different about them, and when confusion and misunderstanding continue, shame continues. We are doing them a great disservice when we make them flounder through school, causing them to think there is something wrong with them.

Do We Call it a Learning Disability or a Learning Difference?

Many individuals with dyslexia have strong opinions when it comes to the label they are given and how differences are perceived. Their opinions are rooted in our inclination to emphasize weaknesses over strengths. Again, this points to our limited view of intelligence. The most valuable opinions should be those who are directly affected.

> What is a disability? Because we can't do math as well as someone else, because we can't read as well, because we read slower, that makes us disabled? But what about the people who can't do art as well as us, or who can't think of things the way we do, or who can't do film work, they're not called disabled. Why not? (Sarah Spier as quoted in Hubbell, 2012)

While it is true that calling dyslexia a learning disability can be necessary to receive remediation outside of the classroom, it is more appropriately described as a learning difference. The difference lies in their unique learning style that requires different teaching strategies, and the recognition of strengths that are not as easily recognized in the school setting. Actually, how we respond is more important than what we call it. If we are optimistic and appreciate what they can offer, they can better accept and deal with their challenges.

Formal Diagnosis versus Informal Screening

A formal diagnosis can only be given by a licensed psychologist, a psychiatrist, or a physician. It involves a comprehensive evaluation consisting of developmental and social history, intelligence testing, achievement testing, visual-motor perceptual tests, and expressive and receptive language testing. Having a diagnosis of dyslexia is important, but it's just the starting point.

The expense of a formal diagnosis and the difficulty of finding qualified testers can be a deterrent for many. Another option is an informal screening, which can be completed by any certified academic language therapist. Screenings can give families a good indication of whether the individual being tested has dyslexia or another learning disability. While screenings don't hold as much authority, they are beneficial for advocating for the person and gaining a better sense of direction.

If college is in the future, a formal diagnosis and documentation showing a plan of accommodations in the student's educational history are necessary. A recently approved plan within twelve months of beginning college makes it possible to receive accommodations on college admissions tests and in the classroom.

Colleges and universities vary in their willingness to make the necessary accommodations for students with learning disabilities despite the legal ramifications of not complying. The same is true of K-12 schools. Although all schools are mandated to provide services and accommodations for learning disabled students through the Americans with Disabilities Act (ADA), some go the extra mile and some do the bare minimum when it comes to providing support.

The most important benefit of receiving either a formal diagnosis or informal screening is gaining knowledge. This leads to a better understanding of how to proceed if you are advocating for someone and a better self-awareness for the individual with dyslexia. Without this, the diagnosis or screening is in vain. Just like going to your family doctor can result in a medical diagnosis accompanied by the necessary treatment, undergoing an evaluation or screening for dyslexia should result in a formal or informal diagnosis accompanied by a treatment plan.

In Summary

The label of dyslexia, if accompanied by all the facts, can be extremely helpful. If the label is masked by myths, misunderstanding, and the narrow perspective that emphasizes only weaknesses, it is hurtful.

I believe children basically want the same thing. They want to be liked, they want to be good at something, and they want to be happy. They need accurate information, encouragement, and a reason to persevere when things are tough. That will keep them moving forward despite the stumbling blocks along the way.

Myth: People with dyslexia can't go to college.
Busted:

> My parents were told that I would be lucky to balance my checkbook and forget college. I have a bachelor's degree and an MBA and run a $30 million business. I am dyslexic—always have been. Wasn't Einstein and Mark Twain also dyslexic? Being different is not the same as dumb—it's just different and we should celebrate it. (Gladwell, 2013)

> From my twenty years of working directly with dyslexic students at Yale and other universities, and from my research and that of others, the 'sea of brilliance interspersed with isolated islands of weakness' model has held up. (Shaywitz, 2003)

10

―◆―

? Change Is Impossible ?
Why Not Move Forward

Sally's Story: Wisdom in Reflection

"I've always wondered if I had 'dilecksia' or if it was just ADD" (attention deficit disorder). "But then, whatever it was, I still wonder if my problems actually helped me. Now that I look back, I consider it a blessing. In my career, the fear of someone finding out my problems was always the motivation that kept me pushing harder." Sally's drive and perseverance, in spite of finding some tasks difficult, was rooted in the positive outlook she personified. Her positivity came from a deeply-imbedded faith that gave her a sense of peace that could banish any fear of someone discovering her differences. Her story is yet another example of how struggle produced strength, made evident when Sally climbed the corporate ladder of AT&T, becoming a second line manager.

As Sally shared how she struggled with reading and writing, and her mispronunciation of the word *dyslexia*, I was inclined to think she is dyslexic. Not only does she fit some of the common indicators, but seeing her perseverance reminds me of so many other dyslexics who fought through when things were tough, refusing to give up. Perseverance is a trait that is more likely to flourish with the discovery of strengths, and Sally has both a healthy acceptance of her weaknesses as well as a good grasp of the strengths that helped her to overcome.

While Sally holds the view that difficulties with reading and writing probably forced her to work harder, she also feels life would have been easier if she had known there was a name and reason for the struggles. She reflects on how past experiences have contributed to a successful career at AT&T despite not completing college. On the other hand, she says, "Not knowing what caused the struggle was so much harder than knowing and dealing with it."

Recognizing that she was good at many things helped Sally push through the struggles and learn to compensate. She found encouragement in her strong math skills, in her ability to memorize, and in an insatiable work ethic. Sally didn't even realize she was having problems until she was in the fifth grade. Prior speech problems did not even ring a bell that she may have learning differences. However, now she realizes that her inability to distinguish sounds played a part in the difficulty to learn to read and write. "I never had a love for reading," Sally adds. Many students hit a wall when they get to fourth and fifth grades because the proportion of words that are irregular, those that do not follow the regular rules for pronunciation, are used in text more frequently. The differences become more pronounced, and learning to compensate becomes a survival strategy.

Sally's fifth grade teacher pointed out a strength that became one of her strongest assets. The affirmation came as a mixed message: the ability to be the best in her class at giving oral reports, while the worst in class at writing reports. The stark difference was surprising to her teacher, yet this is just another indication of dyslexia. As years passed, her natural ability to speak in front of a group played a big part in her promotion to Signature Account Sales Manager at AT&T.

Most positions at AT&T require a college degree, but Sally surpassed coworkers who, in her mind, were smarter and more educated. Her ability to give sales presentations to large business customers, negotiate through obstacles, and her natural people skills became key to climbing the ladder. Sally finds this a miracle since she held a secret only a few select coworkers knew about. She continued to need help with written proposals, another integral part of the job, and relied on a friend to proofread them. Her struggle with written proposals caused great anxiety through the many periods of downsizing and layoffs. "I was afraid every day of getting fired instead of getting promoted." But Sally, like Jeanine, had an ability to "talk her way out of a box."

Sally recalls another childhood memory that helped her develop skills she would use throughout her life. She fondly remembers when her grandmother lived with her family when she was in the second or third grade. Her grandmother's encouragement to tell her all about the Sunday sermon after church led to the discipline of listening and an ease with conversation. Sally loved the way her grandmother would eat up every word and even finish her thoughts, which now she knows was because her grandmother already knew the Bible stories inside and out. Wanting to please her grandmother, she learned to concentrate and listen intently to the sermons and she especially held onto the words of encouragement that Jesus would always be with her.

Having a son who is dyslexic also brought a greater self-awareness, as she saw they shared many similar traits. Sally's son, Tony, "faked reading through second grade." But Tony, like his mother, had a work ethic that caused him to push through when school was tough, including college. He also had the ability to negotiate and "talk his way out of a box." He used this ability when he had to convince his professors that he should be allowed into the Master's Program for Marketing. Grades alone would not get him into the program, but the gift of persuasion and hard work was the ticket in. Ultimately, this led to getting his dream job.

An added bonus to meeting Sally was learning that her daughter, a teacher in Michigan, teaches STEAM class to grades K-5. This program is an innovative way to reach our dyslexic students who often excel in the five subjects its letters signify and the methods used to teach.

> STEAM is an educational approach to learning that uses Science, Technology, Engineering, the Arts and Mathematics as access points for guiding student inquiry, dialogue, and critical thinking. The end results are students who take thoughtful risks, engage in experiential learning, persist in problem-solving, embrace collaboration, and work through the creative process. These are the innovators, educators, leaders, and learners of the 21st century! (http://educationcloset.com/steam/what-is-steam)

In light of the fact that many dyslexic students excel in visual-spatial and three-dimensional skills as well as creativity and imagination, this could be the perfect outlet for demonstrating strengths. Watching excited children build and operate robots, create architectural masterpieces, and construct scientific experiments that satisfy the curious mind is truly inspirational. Tony's observation after learning about his sister's STEAM class was, "I wish we had something like that when I was in school."

Sally's motivation for sharing her story is similar to others' within this book. She wants to see more understanding for those who have different learning needs. Not sympathy, because that would mean only looking at weaknesses, but a recognition of the strengths that are so often ignored. She just wants to be understood with the same understanding extended to others.

Reflections of early experiences in school, at home, and working at AT&T were rooted in a positive attitude that kept her focusing on strengths over weaknesses. Her grandmother gave her the motivation to learn to concentrate when it was not necessarily a natural gift. But she gave her much more than that. She instilled one of her life philosophies, a belief system that would forever shape Sally's life. "It's all in our attitude, in the way we deal with things—to make things work rather than having a defeatist attitude." This philosophy has guided her life and given her the momentum required to succeed. Sally's philosophy can be just the inspiration needed to turn a defeated attitude into an optimistic outlook.

Where Do We Go From Here?

"Unless someone like you cares a whole awful lot, nothing is going to get better. It's not." This book was launched with these words from Dr. Seuss's *The Lorax*. My motivation for sharing stories of those with dyslexia, as well as facts to help us move forward, is that I care. I invite you to care also. I invite you to be another voice for the misunderstood child with dyslexia: the child whose gifts are squelched, the child who feels all alone in his differences, the child who just wants to know why he can't learn like others.

The first step is knowledge, and you are taking that step by reading this book. But don't stop there! Learn about resources in your area. Just by googling "dyslexia resources in my area," you can open the door to getting help. Then go deeper and find out if the resource you're looking at uses strategies that are backed by research. Find ways to explore strengths giving opportunities for outlets to express them.

In the process of caring, I had to face head-on the frustrations of that faceless giant called our educational system and realize that continuing to just complain about it and wish it would change was futile. While the system is moving forward in some areas, we are decades behind in other areas. Our traditional way of doing things is preventing us from hearing the cries of millions of children.

For awhile, I asked the questions, "Why can't we address what the dyslexic child really needs? And why can't I call it what it is—dyslexia?" The spoken and unspoken answers: "That's not how we do it" or "That's not what we call it." The questions were met with what felt like a reprimand of *stop rocking the boat and just do your job!*

Eventually, I fell into the state of mind that many teachers are in today—that sinking feeling that you just can't quite keep your head above water. It becomes about survival, and many times the decision has to be made if our energy will go toward students or the menagerie of other expectations. Do we invest our energy into learning the newly improved "best" curriculum; professional development that sometimes is relevant and sometimes isn't; the ever-increasing paperwork; and, of course, the newest technology craze? Or do we invest in students, finding what works for all the varying learning differences, nurturing relationships so they want to learn, and learning what makes them tick? The only way it's possible to do both is to work sixty plus hours a week, and that may not be enough.

The question for me became, "Do I continue to keep the status quo and try to positively impact a few children within the system?" or "Do I take a risk with the hope to reach a wider audience by writing a book?" I chose to become one voice speaking out on behalf of those who are so misunderstood, and with this decision is an inner assurance that some of you will join me on this advocacy road.

But even more important than reaching those who can become advocates, I hope to be a source of encouragement to those with dyslexia. Actually, it is not I, but the courageous, gifted individuals who shared their stories that can bring hope and a sense of direction. Their practical advice, their determination to do whatever it takes to succeed, and their discovery of gifts are just a few tips for those still enduring the constant reminder of learning differences.

The philosophy of Sally's grandmother can become our way of thinking. She instilled in her granddaughter the attitude of doing whatever it takes to make things work rather than sinking into a defeatist attitude.

One of the challenges I propose to our education system is to explore what intelligence is. In this day and age of advanced technology, can we really justify the narrow view that paper/pencil tasks give us? Do we really think filling in the computer-generated, multiple-choice dot gives us any indication of how the right-brain-dominant individual is processing information? Is it really fair to continue with this line of thinking when our society is making huge advancements in technology?

Another challenge I address to both our educators and those who are impacted by dyslexia: discover what makes the individual with dyslexia tick? Not just what's wrong with them, but what's *right* with them. The information is out there, we just have to take the time to explore the truth. Exploring what dyslexia looks like and how children and adults are impacted by it is important, but to positively influence the struggling learner, we have to search out what works. In this book, we looked at the Orton-Gillingham approach along with the five components of reading instruction and the research behind them. The number of individuals who need advocates far outnumber those who will step up to the challenge.

Finally, I challenge all of us to stop limiting ourselves and others with preconceived thinking. We limit by thinking only the student who falls in what we call "the norm" should go to college. We are limited by fear of failure. We are limited by believing our inner dialogue and the haunting voices from the past that tell us we aren't good enough.

The challenges I propose are not necessarily easy, but the joy of seeing lives transformed is more rewarding than the time and effort invested. It can be as simple as recognizing strengths to as complex as fighting for a child's rights in the classroom.

I have chosen to move forward. I ask you to join me on this road of advocacy—speaking out for those who are too wounded or defeated to do it themselves. I ask you to make a positive impact in the life of a child who learns differently.

I choose to care! Do you?

Myth: We can't overcome past mistakes and injustices. Busted:

> Although she had to endure bullying and name calling during her school years, Whoopi credits those who criticized her with giving her the motivation to succeed. She says that they "went into making me the sum total of what I became, and what I've become."(www.dyslexia-reading-well.com/whoopi-goldberg.html)

REFERENCES

Eide, Brock L. and Eide, Fernette F. 2011. *The Dyslexic Advantage: Unlocking the Hidden Potential of the Dyslexic Brain.* New York: The Penguin Group

Gladwell, Malcolm. 2013. *David and Goliath: Underdogs, Misfits, and the Art of Battling Giants.* New York: Little, Brown and Company

Hubbell, Harvey V. 2012. *Dislecksia: The Book.* North Charleston, SC: CreateSpace Independent Publishing Platform

Laughlin, Davis. 2013. *Ripple Maker.* Benton, KS: Davis Laughlin, Ltd.

Milner, Steven. 2012. *Dyslexia Way of Thinking.* Bayern, Germany: JF Marketing Concepts

Moats, Louisa Cook and Dakin, Karen E. 2008. *Basic Facts about Dyslexia and Other Reading Problems.* Baltimore, MD: The International Dyslexia Association

Shaywitz, Sally. 2003. *Overcoming Dyslexia: a New and Complete Science-based Program for Reading Problems at Any Level.* New York: Alfred A. Knopf, a division of Random House

Schultz, Philip. 2011. *My Dyslexia.* New York: W.W. Norton & Company